THE SUPREMES'
GREATEST HITS

 ★ 2ND REVISED & UPDATED EDITION ★

★ ★ ★

THE SUPREMES' GREATEST HITS

★ 2ND REVISED & UPDATED EDITION ★

THE 44 SUPREME COURT CASES
THAT MOST DIRECTLY AFFECT YOUR LIFE

★ ★ ★

MICHAEL G. TRACHTMAN

STERLING
New York

STERLING
New York

An Imprint of Sterling Publishing Co., Inc.
1166 Avenue of the Americas
New York, NY 10036

© 2007, 2009, 2016 Michael G. Trachtman

ISBN 978-1-4549-2077-9

Distributed in Canada by Sterling Publishing Co., Inc.
C/o Canadian Manda Group, 664 Annette Street
Toronto, Ontario, M6S 2C8, Canada
Distributed in the United Kingdom by GMC Distribution Services
Castle Place, 166 High Street, Lewes, East Sussex, BN7 1XU, England
Distributed in Australia by NewSouth Books
45 Beach Street, Coogee, NSW 2034, Australia

For information about custom editions, special sales, and premium
and corporate purchases, please contact Sterling Special Sales at 800-805-5489
or specialsales@sterlingpublishing.com.

Manufactured in Canada

6 8 10 9 7 5

sterlingpublishing.com

CONTENTS

CHAPTER 6
THE RIGHT TO DO WHAT YOU WANT

CHAPTER 7
"BIG GOVERNMENT" IN YOUR BUSINESS AND YOUR BACKYARD

ACKNOWLEDGMENTS

It was John Boswell's idea that this book should be written, and that I should be the one to write it. I am extremely grateful for his creativity and generosity, and for the help he has freely given me in my effort to fulfill his vision.

The book would not have been possible without Sterling Publishing's willingness to support and expertly assist my chosen approach to this subject matter, and I am most appreciative of the fact that Sterling has partnered with me to update the book as the Supreme Court moves through one of the most consequential periods in its history. In particular, my editor, Barbara Berger, has been a source of encouragement and expertise, and I wish to thank her for, among many other things, helping me to bridge the cavernous gap between being a lawyer and being an author.

Lawyers sometimes forget how to write and think like non-lawyers. My wife, Jen, provided invaluable simultaneous translation services as I struggled to overcome those disabilities. Many apologies to her and my son, Ben, for the attention paid to this manuscript at their expense, and many more thanks for their understanding and encouragement.

AUTHOR'S NOTE

I have made some admittedly arbitrary and subjective decisions respecting which Supreme Court cases deserve to be included in the forty-four cases that are featured in this book. Many cases, while of great importance within the context of a specific legal issue, do not have a broader societal impact. There are cases that may seem significant now, but are likely to fade over time. And there are cases that fall into gray areas that require difficult judgment calls. I have done my best to apply these and a myriad of other criteria to the task.

My decisions are, certainly, subject to what would be a healthy and (at least for me) enjoyable debate. For example, *National Federation of Independent Businesses v. Sebelius* (2012) established (in a convoluted way) the constitutionality of the core provisions of the Affordable Care Act—"Obamacare"—but beyond that, it did not secure the future of Obamacare or establish or clarify constitutional principles that will substantially influence the law beyond that immediate result. Similarly, in *Shelby County v. Holder* (2013), the Supreme Court overturned a provision of the Voting Rights Act that had prohibited nine states with a history of discriminatory voting practices from changing their election procedures without approval by the federal government—an important decision for voters in those states but, most likely, not a decision that will have a major impact on the law outside of that context.

Once the forty-four cases were selected, I struggled to objectively explain and analyze them, as well as the competing viewpoints they have engendered. I have also struggled to base my criticisms of judicial opinions and approaches on law and logic, and not on my personal viewpoints. I will consider those struggles to have been a success if this book equips the reader with enough information and insight to tell me how and why I failed.

INTRODUCTION

"A GOVERNMENT OF LAWS, NOT MEN"

High school civics students are taught that our system of government is composed of three branches: the legislature makes the laws; the executive enforces the laws; and the courts interpret the laws. As for the Supreme Court, they know that it is the highest court in the land—the final word on legal disputes.

So far as it goes, all of this is true. But to describe the Supreme Court in this way is to describe champagne as grape juice, or the Grand Canyon as a river valley—accurate to a point, but so shallow and incomplete as to be grotesquely misleading. Over 175 years ago, Alexis de Tocqueville, the celebrated French political observer, studied the Supreme Court and concluded, "A more imposing judicial power was never constituted by any people." The same holds true today.

The Ultimate Check and Balance: "Judicial Review"

Like the highest courts of other democracies, the Supreme Court has the authority to decide, once and for all, what important laws really mean when applied to the real-life situations that arise after the laws are enacted. Does the Civil Rights Act of 1964 protect women against sexual harassment? Does the Americans with Disabilities Act cover people with certain heart conditions? Various lower courts disagreed. The Supreme Court interpreted the wording and intent of the statutes and made a ruling. End of controversy.

But the most momentous role the Supreme Court plays in our society extends well beyond interpreting statutes: The Supreme Court serves as the ultimate interpreter and protector of our most fundamental rights—the rights set forth in the Constitution. Most historians agree that the American Constitution is the oldest national constitution still in effect, and it has stood the test of time for a reason. The framers of the Constitution drafted a document that was definitive in many respects, but also sufficiently vague so that it could be applied to unimaginable, changing circumstances. The framers of the Constitution knew things would change—as, of course, they did: No one could have anticipated the industrial revolution, or the aftermath of slavery, or World War II, or the Internet. They needed a mechanism to breathe continuing life into the Constitution. They needed, and therefore created, the Supreme Court.

The Supreme Court keeps the Constitution alive in two related ways. First, in the same way it interprets statutes, it interprets the Constitution. Does the First Amendment right of free speech allow you to burn the flag as a political statement? Does the Constitution's "Commerce Clause" allow Congress to outlaw racial discrimination, or Internet pornography? Supreme Court justices decide these issues, and the myriad of other questions that define our rights and lifestyles, through a process that is both rooted in historical precedent and at the same time highly intuitive and dependent on individual value judgments and philosophies. Through it all, the goal is to somehow determine what a group of eighteenth-century scholars, farmers, businessmen, soldiers, and politicians really meant by the words they wrote, and what they would have done if faced with a twenty-first century they could not have hoped to envision.

The second way the Supreme Court empowers the Constitution is what stupefied de Tocqueville and so many others who have studied our democracy: the Supreme Court has the authority to decide that any act of a government official, and any law passed by a government body, violates the Constitution and is therefore invalid and of no effect. This power, termed the power of "judicial review," is virtually limitless. It encompasses the right to void the decisions of township officials, mayors, governors, and the president of the United States. It includes the right to strike from the books any township ordinance, state law, or Act of Congress. Supreme Court justices are appointed for life and, therefore, do not have to worry about making the popular decision, as opposed to the right decision. They can just say no.

This is a remarkable aspect of the American way of life. Through its proper exercise, the Supreme Court can ensure that it is the Constitution—not the people who happen to populate the Congress or the White House or the local city hall at any given time—that defines the extent to which our property and liberty can be compromised by our government.

This ultimate check and balance makes us what billions of people in the world strive to be—what John Adams first called a "government of laws, not men."

The Supreme Court has not been shy about using its authority. At times, the Supreme Court justices have made decisions that were welcomed when they were handed down, but are now seen as horrifically wrong, even repugnant. At other times, they have made decisions that were reviled, but are now seen as bastions of freedom and wisdom. Either way, it is difficult to overstate the influence the Supreme Court wields. The Supreme Court desegregated American schools. The Supreme Court allowed the internment of Japanese-Americans during World War II. The Supreme Court decided who you may, and may not, refuse to serve or hire in your restaurant or accounting firm. The Supreme Court decided what your rights will be if your supervisor sexually harasses you. The Supreme Court decreed and defined the right to an abortion. The Supreme Court decided how the forty-third president of the United States would be elected. The Supreme Court defined the role of money in politics. The Supreme Court determined when your town council may appropriate your backyard and make it a parking lot for a shopping mall. The Supreme Court defined your right to carry a gun.

And it will be the Supreme Court that will resolve the hot-button issues of the twenty-first century. To what extent may the right to an abortion be regulated? Will your school board be permitted to require your child to study "intelligent design" over your objection? What restrictions will be permitted on "the right to bear arms"? To what extent will the federal government be permitted to monitor your e-mails, location, cell phone, and bank accounts in the name of national security? How far can we go in the effort to effectively limit the influence of corporate money in American elections? How will we deal with the myriad of issues, some known and many yet to be discovered, that the Internet and related technologies will present?

There is no appeal from a Supreme Court decision. It speaks last.

It is not surprising that the appointment of a Supreme Court justice stirs passions, argument, and multimillion-dollar lobbying efforts—few persons in our society have more power to define how we live.

What Exactly Is the Constitution?

During the Revolutionary War, the colonies were bound together through the Articles of Confederation, which created a very loose central government composed only of Congress. Because there was no national president or judiciary, Congress had no way to enforce what it decreed, and it was left to the various states to comply on, essentially, a voluntary basis. The states were often less than cooperative, and many sought to compete, rather than cooperate, with each other. It was obvious that the colonies would never become a "nation" under the

Articles, and this reality created the impetus for the Constitutional Convention in Philadelphia, at which the Constitution was drafted in 1787. The Constitution then had to be ratified by each of the states, a process that took two years of contentious proceedings, after which the Constitution became effective in 1789.

The Constitution is, by its own words, the "supreme law of the land." Most of the Constitution deals with the creation of a federal government—establishing the three branches; defining their powers; and, very important to the framers, limiting their powers. Several of the cases discussed later focus on the national crises that have accompanied the battles among the branches of government, and the battles among the federal government and the states over the limits of their respective spheres of authority. It is always left to the Supreme Court to interpret the Constitution and resolve these potential fractures in the system—as, for example, when Truman took it upon himself to seize the steel industry during the Korean War, or when Nixon refused to turn over his tapes to Congress in the Watergate scandal.

The Bill of Rights

The Bill of Rights is composed of the first ten amendments to the Constitution. The fear among many of the Founding Fathers and many of the states was that the central government created by the Constitution could become tyrannical if the people were not guaranteed certain basic rights. Spurred by those concerns, within a few years after the Constitution was adopted, the Bill of Rights, encompassing many of our most fundamental bedrock freedoms, was finalized and ratified by the states. As Justice Robert H. Jackson once explained it, "The very purpose of a Bill of Rights was to withdraw certain subjects from the vicissitudes of political controversy, to place them beyond the reach of majorities and officials and to establish them as legal principles to be applied by the courts."

The essence of the Bill of Rights is set forth below.

FIRST AMENDMENT: This amendment prohibits the government from making any laws "respecting an establishment of religion," or prohibiting "the free exercise" of religion, or "abridging the freedom of speech." The First Amendment also protects the right of the people to assemble and petition the government for redress of grievances.

SECOND AMENDMENT: This amendment includes the often-quoted "right of the people to keep and bear arms."

THIRD AMENDMENT: This amendment, a reaction to the way in which the British treated the colonists, provides that no soldier shall be quartered in any house without the consent of the owner.

FOURTH AMENDMENT: This amendment protects the people against "unreasonable searches and seizures" by the government and requires that warrants be issued only on probable cause, and with specificity.

FIFTH AMENDMENT: This amendment provides a multitude of rights. It defines how certain indictments must issue. It protects people against "double jeopardy" (that is, being tried twice for the same crime). It provides the right against self-incrimination. It provides that persons may not be "deprived of life, liberty, or property, without due process of law." And it provides that private property may be taken by the government for public use, but that just compensation must be paid.

SIXTH AMENDMENT: This amendment provides criminal defendants with the right to a speedy and public trial by an impartial jury. It also provides a defendant with the right to be informed of the charges made, to confront the witnesses against him, to subpoena his own witnesses, and to have the assistance of counsel.

SEVENTH AMENDMENT: This amendment provides for the right to a jury trial in certain civil cases.

EIGHTH AMENDMENT: This amendment prohibits "cruel and unusual punishment" and forbids excessive bail and excessive fines.

NINTH AMENDMENT: This amendment clarifies that although the Constitution provides certain rights to the people, it is not to be interpreted as diminishing all of the other rights the people have under the law—in other words, the Constitution is not the only source of the people's rights.

TENTH AMENDMENT: This amendment provides that all rights not delegated by the Constitution to the federal government are to be retained by the states or the people.

A great many Supreme Court cases focus on the effort to define and protect the rights of Americans as set forth in the Bill of Rights—and what to do when those rights conflict with one another. Several of those cases are discussed in the chapters that follow.

The Fourteenth Amendment

The Fourteenth Amendment to the Constitution was passed in 1868. It includes various sections, but the most renowned section includes the provisions known as the "Due Process Clause" and the "Equal Protection Clause," which guarantee basic freedoms that, like the Bill of Rights, have been continuing focal points for the Supreme Court: "No State shall make or enforce any law which shall abridge the privileges or immunities of citizens of the United States; nor shall any State deprive any person of life, liberty, or property, without due process of law; nor deny to any person within its jurisdiction the equal protection of the laws."

The specific wording of the Bill of Rights prohibited the *federal* government, but not the *state* governments, from compromising fundamental freedoms. The Fourteenth Amendment was enacted in the wake of the Emancipation Proclamation in order to make it clear that, at the very least, the states owed constitutional duties of due process and equal protection to all persons. Ultimately, the Fourteenth Amendment was interpreted by the Supreme Court to require that the states also respect the core provisions of the Bill of Rights, such as free speech, the free exercise of religion, the right to counsel, and so on.

Particularly in the twentieth century, the Supreme Court has addressed numerous issues arising from the reluctance of some states to comply with notions of due process and equal protection and to fairly apply the Bill of Rights. This has led to colossal societal changes, such as desegregation, restrictions on the role of religion in schools and government, and the rights of the accused. Some of the most important of these cases are explained in the chapters that follow.

How the Supreme Court Works

The cases in this book illuminate how the Supreme Court has interpreted the Constitution and used its power of judicial review to define, and redefine, our way of life. To better understand how these cases came to be decided, it helps to understand what the Supreme Court is and how it goes about its business.

The Supreme Court is composed of a chief justice and eight associate justices, all of whom are nominated by the president and confirmed with the "advice and consent" of the Senate. The senatorial confirmation process entails a detailed investigation, a lengthy Judiciary Committee hearing, and a full Senate vote. Particularly in the last twenty years, Senate confirmation has become a harrowing experience, drawing extensive television coverage and well-funded lobbying efforts reinforced by major media campaigns. The politicization of the process was amply demonstrated after the 2016 death of Justice Scalia, when the Senate majority leader and Judiciary Committee chair quickly announced that they would not so much as consider President Obama's nominee until a new president was inaugurated in 2017, effectively emasculating the Court's ability to decide close cases in the interim.

Presidents typically nominate someone they believe will share their political and judicial philosophies, but the history of the Supreme Court is replete with justices who were supposed to be of one stripe, and turned out to be much different. A lifetime appointment to a position with the power to change fundamental rights and national policies, free from direct political pressures, can easily change one's perspective and ideology.

President Eisenhower, for instance, appointed Chief Justice Earl Warren, believing that he would be a conservative jurist. Warren turned out to be one of the most liberal and activist chief justices in history, prompting Eisenhower to call the appointment "the biggest damn-fool mistake I ever made." When Justice David Souter was nominated in 1990, the National Organization of Women, believing he would seek to overturn Roe v. Wade, distributed flyers blaring "Stop Souter or Women Will Die." After he was confirmed, Justice Souter helped write the opinion reaffirming the continuing validity of Roe v. Wade.

In rare instances, such as boundary-line disputes between states, the litigants have a right to bring their claim directly to the Supreme Court. Otherwise, the Supreme Court gets to choose the cases it hears. After a case has been decided by a lower state or federal court, a litigant has the right to file a petition with the Supreme Court seeking a "writ of certiorari," the technical term for the writ the Supreme Court issues when it agrees to hear and decide an appeal.

Typically, the Court will consider something in the neighborhood of seven to eight thousand such petitions a year. In the selection process, the justices look for cases of constitutional significance and other matters of national importance. After an initial screening process that eliminates most of the petitions, the justices meet to consider the remaining petitions on Wednesdays and Fridays in a secure conference room, in which no outsiders are allowed. The justices study the petitions well in advance of this conference, and, after the chief justice opens the discussion by summarizing each case, each justice then speaks, in order of seniority. The most junior justice has the task of guarding the door: if reference material or anything else is needed, the junior justice notifies an attendant stationed outside of the conference room, and then, outside the door, receives whatever was requested. No one enters the room.

It takes a vote of four justices to "grant cert," as it is colloquially called. If "cert" is not granted, the decision of the lower court remains undisturbed. From the thousands of petitions for certiorari it receives each year, the current Court typically accepts about eighty cases on which it renders written decisions.

Each Supreme Court term begins on the first Monday in October. Well before each Court session, the lawyers representing the parties submit detailed briefs, which the justices carefully study. During Court sessions, which are open to the public, the lawyers present oral arguments to the justices. Frequently, individual justices will interrupt and ask the lawyers difficult and pointed questions, sometimes for the purpose of honestly exploring the merits of an issue, sometimes for the purpose of reinforcing a favored position or tearing down a disfavored position in the hope of building support among the other justices.

After oral arguments, a conference is scheduled, at which the justices discuss and vote on how they believe a case should be decided, at least at that point. If the chief justice is in the majority, he assigns either himself or another justice to write the majority opinion; if not, the senior justice who is in the majority makes that assignment. Other justices may write their own concurring or dissenting opinions. The opinions are then circulated among the justices in the effort to build as much consensus as possible. Debates continue, and opinions are revised, as the justices continue to exchange views among themselves.

Ultimately, each justice decides whether he or she will subscribe to the majority opinion. A justice who votes with the majority may also write a concurring opinion, explaining his or her own views. Justices who do not subscribe to the majority view may write dissenting opinions to explain the bases for their position. Most cases are decided clearly and decisively, but approximately twenty to thirty percent of the cases carry only a 5–4 majority. As will be discussed in the note to the 2nd Revised & Updated Edition, in recent years many of the Court's most significant 5–4 decisions have been characterized by a troubling consistency: two voting blocs have emerged—one bloc composed of four justices appointed by Republican presidents, and the other of four justices appointed by Democratic presidents, with Justice Kennedy acting as the deciding, "swing" vote. Some cases are so difficult and contentious that they generate numerous opinions, none of which garners the support of a majority.

What if the Supreme Court Issued an Order . . . and No One Listened?

It is frequently said that the Supreme Court has no army—a pithy way to make the point that the Supreme Court has no way to independently enforce its rulings. Consequently, the Court depends on the will of the other branches of government, usually the president, to carry out its decisions, as when troops were called in to enforce school desegregation after *Brown v. Board of Education*.

We take it for granted that what the Supreme Court says, goes. Still, there are nightmare scenarios that are difficult to contemplate. As many of the cases in the following chapters demonstrate, sometimes the Supreme Court has to take on the president head-on, and sometimes a true reading of the Constitution requires the Court to take an extremely unpopular position. If a president openly defied a Supreme Court order, what then? If the president were backed by the polls, would Congress have the political will to pursue impeachment in order to protect the Constitution? Would the Supreme Court, as many fear, devolve into partisan politics?

These are the kinds of upheavals that plague countries without engrained constitutional traditions, where might makes right. At least for now, our tradition and culture make these scenarios unlikely; respect for the highest court's interpretation of the Constitution is, after all, at the root of what defines "a government of laws, not men."

But whether this remains the case will depend on whether the justices are viewed, beyond rational doubt, as serving only the Constitution, and not their own political agendas or social or religious philosophies. If the good faith of those who make up the Supreme Court ever comes into serious question, the moral authority of the Court—which is, really, the only authority the Court ultimately has—will evaporate, with disastrous results.

The following chapters explain some of the Supreme Court decisions that have had the greatest impact on our history and character, and that most affect the everyday lives of Americans. The intention is to enable the reader to appreciate the mammoth difficulty and consequence of the issues the Supreme Court has had to wrestle with, and to allow the reader to reach an informed judgment on whether the Supreme Court has earned its moral authority.

Some of these decisions resonate from the past; others deal exclusively with twenty-first-century issues; all of them help define who we are and where we are going. They illuminate the tensions between individual liberty and the interests of society, the challenge of balancing majority rule with minority rights, the difficulties of applying old laws to new technologies and changing cultures, and the need to address crises in the short term while preserving fundamental rights in the long term. Like it or not, each of us, and our children who come after us, will be affected, even transformed, by what these decisions say.

THE DANGER——AND THE POST-SCALIA FUTURE—— OF THE ROBERTS COURT'S 5-4 DECISIONS

"It is confidence in the men and women who administer the judicial system that is the true backbone of the rule of law."

—JOHN PAUL STEVENS,
ASSOCIATE SUPREME COURT JUSTICE, 1975–2010

During the first few years after Chief Justice John G. Roberts was appointed in 2005, and on an accelerating basis since the publication of the first Revised & Updated Edition of this book in 2009, the Supreme Court has been criticized, sometimes denounced, for its 5–4 decisions, especially in important cases that garner public attention. Many of those cases are explained in the following chapters. The criticism has been egalitarian—it comes from the left and the right, from Supreme Court scholars and ordinary citizens. It is an issue that demands careful analysis, especially right now.

The Law of the Land . . . By One Vote

A 5–4 vote is a scary proposition that highlights just how important an appointment to the Supreme Court can be. If *one* justice saw things

Portrait of the Roberts Court taken on October 8, 2010, on the occasion of Justice Elena Kagan's joining the Court.

differently, for example, Al Gore might have been president, Obamacare might not have gotten off the ground, and the lines between church and state would likely be much different than they are today.

The issue is not whether the Roberts Court issues more 5–4 decisions than many prior Courts—in fact, it does not. And there is nothing intrinsically wrong with a 5–4 Supreme Court decision. The Supreme Court deals with close, difficult questions over which justices can reasonably disagree. On the plus side, a 5–4 Supreme Court decision, usually replete with an array of majority and dissenting opinions, can establish and clarify the rationales on both sides of a thorny and important legal and societal issue, and provide the foundation on which future Supreme Court justices can inch constitutional law forward, a crucial step at a time—like a medical study or physics theorem that provides a foundation for future researchers to understand and debunk, or verify and utilize, prior hypotheses in the painstaking search for an answer.

Still, there is another aspect: Unlike a *developing* study or *proposed* theorem that affects the evolution of future research, the moment a 5–4 decision is issued, it becomes a concrete, societal reality that can affect the lives of hundreds of millions of people. The sheer reach and power of many Supreme Court decisions, 5–4 or otherwise, stirs intense debate and controversy, and will often prompt politicians and commentators (and, sometimes, dissenting Supreme Court justices) to rail about why "nine unelected justices" should be able to wield such authority.

That question has a surface appeal, until the alternative is considered: if unelected Supreme Court justices do not make these tough calls, who will? John Adams warned of the "tyranny of the majority"—one of the bedrock precepts of the Constitution, especially the Bill of Rights, is to insulate our fundamental freedoms from the whims and prejudices of majority rule. This is why, at least theoretically, nine unelected Supreme Court justices are particularly well positioned to rise above polls and politics and focus on what is constitutional, as opposed to what shifting election year positions they need to take to curry favor with the most voters.

And this is also why so many of the 5–4 votes of the Roberts Court have threatened this vital aspect of our constitutional fabric.

The Perception of Partisanship

The Roberts Court's 5–4 decisions have been different, and dangerous. In the majority of the Roberts Court's most consequential 5–4 decisions, the same four "conservative" justices, *all appointed by Republican presidents,* join together on one side; the same four "liberal" justices, *all appointed by Democratic presidents,* join together on the other side; and Justice Kennedy, part Republican conservative, part libertarian, becomes a one-man Supreme Court with the authority to tilt the balance one way or the other.

There is nothing at all wrong with a justice having strong and consistent viewpoints on principles of constitutional law and interpretation. But it is altogether something else when, year after year, sometimes decade after decade, those viewpoints on constitutional law and interpretation produce a voting record that is suspiciously consistent with the social policy planks in the political platform of the party with which the justice is affiliated. Consider the decisions on campaign finance reform, gun control, same-sex marriage, religious freedom, abortion rights, death penalty for juveniles, and many more. In past decades, predicting how the justices would line up on controversial issues was generally a risky business. Now, particularly in cases involving social-policy issues, the only real challenge is trying to predict what Justice Kennedy will do.

The point is not whether this voting pattern evidences judicial misbehavior or nefarious intentions. Rather, the point is that, as was discussed in the Introduction, in order for the Supreme Court to function in the delicate balance of our democracy, Supreme Court justices must be perceived as being open-minded, focused on the merits of each particular case and, certainly, above politics—and contrary to those ideals, whether or not true, the Roberts Court's voting pattern smacks of partisanship. Indeed, the political parties have used the idea that Supreme Court justices can be expected to cast predictable votes in support of a partisan social agenda as a means to garner votes. If you vote Democratic, future Supreme Court justices will overrule *Citizens United* and reinstate gun control. If you vote Republican, future Supreme Court justices will overrule Obamacare and severely limit *Roe v. Wade*. The Senate's refusal to even consider President Obama's appointment to replace Justice Scalia has further entrenched in the public mind that a Supreme Court justice is, really, just another political appointee who can be expected to do what the president who appointed him or her desires.

Not surprisingly, the perceived politicization of the Supreme Court has resulted in a steady erosion of public confidence in the Court. According to Gallup, in June 2015 (well before the post-Scalia Senate battle), 23 percent of those surveyed trusted the Supreme Court "very little." In June 2000, only 14 percent had harbored those doubts. In June 2015, 32 percent trusted the Supreme Court a "great deal" or "quite a lot." In June 2000, 46 percent had trusted the Court. The number of people who do not trust the Court rose by 64 percent from the number in the 2000 poll, and the number of people who do trust the Court dropped by 30 percent from the number just fifteen years earlier.

All of this brings with it the potential to fracture the bedrock on which any constitutional democracy is built. A lack of trust engenders suspicion and, in this case, the suspicion is that, in important respects, we may be a government of men, and not laws. No one can predict where, if unchecked, that degree of attitudinal shift will lead.

What Will This Mean for the Future of the Supreme Court?

Justice Scalia's passing underlines an actuarial truth: the average age of current Supreme Court justices is close to a record high. Justice Ginsburg was born in 1933. Justice Kennedy was born in 1936. Justice Breyer was born in 1938. Historically, the average retirement age for Supreme Court justices has been about eighty. The next president, and the next president's successor, will very likely have the opportunity to substantially change the nature and trajectory of the Court for a generation.

Despite recent history, however, it is not easy for a president to appoint a tailor-made Supreme Court justice. Often, Supreme Court appointees have surprised the presidents who appointed them, changing their points of view and forging new and unpredictable alliances.

Still, it is possible for a president to find and appoint a nominee whose record indicates a strident, unyielding, and issue-oriented approach. But to join the Court, the nominee would have to secure the approval of a majority of the Senate—or perhaps 60 percent, which would be the vote needed to overcome a filibuster. The court of public opinion will also play a role. The media attention commanded by the Senate "advise and consent" process tends to dissuade any president from appointing a nominee with a clear jurisprudential bias—presidents do not want to be perceived as attempting to stack the Supreme Court deck. This trends in favor of nominees who *seem* more willing to straddle ideological fences, and, beyond generalities, that makes it difficult to predict what positions those nominees will take in the future.

However, aside from the difficulty in discerning the long-term proclivities of a particular nominee, a very important prediction can be made: With Justice Scalia's departure, and with the likelihood of at least one or two more departures over the next one or two presidential terms, the probability of two predictable four-justice voting blocs remaining in place is remote, and that shift will drastically change the dynamic of the Court for the foreseeable future. What will emerge in place of the current Court division, and whether future justices will erase the partisan suspicions that have arisen from the Court's recent past, is beyond the realm of rational forecasting. That uncertainty raises the stakes for future elections and heightens the need for an informed citizenry.

This edition of *The Supremes' Greatest Hits* includes the most impactful decisions of the Roberts Court, along with those prior cases (many of which have been updated) that continue to define how the Supreme Court affects our everyday lives. These will hopefully provide the background and perspective that will enable the reader to assess and understand not only where the Court has been, but the wisdom or folly of where it goes during what promises to be one of the most critical periods in the Supreme Court's history.

CHAPTER 1

HOW THE SUPREME COURT BECAME SUPREME

"We are not final because we are infallible,
but we are infallible only because we are final."

—ROBERT H. JACKSON, SUPREME COURT JUSTICE, 1941–54

The Supreme Court was not always so supreme. It took the Supreme Court's own decision to create this prerogative — in effect, the Supreme Court created its own preeminence.

This seminal decision was rendered in the 1803 case of *Marbury v. Madison*, which gave the Supreme Court the right of "judicial review" — the power, mentioned previously, to determine what is and is not constitutional, and the coordinate right to void governmental actions and laws if they violate the Constitution. This power to ensure compliance with the Constitution not only defined the landscape of our own democracy, it served as a model for constitutional democracies throughout the world.

As would ultimately be seen, however, the power to decide takes with it the power to decide wrongly. And the impact of a wrong decision by the Supreme Court can change the face of society, reverberating for decades, even centuries.

Portraits of influential chief justices of the Supreme Court are depicted in a c. 1894 print. Clockwise from top left: John Jay, John Rutledge, Oliver Ellsworth, Roger B. Taney, Melville W. Fuller, Morrison R. Waite, Salmon P. Chase, and John Marshall.

1. The Birth of a Unique Democracy

Marbury v. Madison (1803)

Marbury v. Madison arose from the uncertainties that characterized the first years after the Constitution was ratified—no one could be sure of exactly what the Constitution would come to mean in practice, and the branches of government openly jockeyed for position. As for the Supreme Court, the framers had not specifically delineated how much influence it should have, and this issue provoked much debate and disagreement. Many felt that the most the Supreme Court could do was interpret laws, not overrule them. Indeed, in the early days of our country, the Supreme Court did not even have its own building (Congress graciously allowed it to conduct business in an unused committee room in the basement of the Capitol), and its role as an equal—let alone preeminent—branch of government was anything but plain.

The seeds of change, however, were planted in 1800, when Republican Thomas Jefferson defeated incumbent Federalist John Adams in a bitterly contested election. Just before he left office, Adams attempted to entrench Federalist judges in the judiciary by appointing sixteen new circuit judges and forty-two new justices of the peace. However, due to a last-minute administrative mix-up as Adams left and Jefferson arrived, one of the appointees, Marbury, did not receive his written commission appointing him as a justice of the peace, even though it had been signed by then-president Adams and confirmed by the Senate.

Jefferson and the Republicans bore much hostility toward the Federalists; and Jefferson, flexing his political muscles and testing the boundaries of presidential power, refused to issue the commission to Marbury. In effect, Jefferson declared that he had the power to do what he pleased, and he dared Marbury to do something about it.

David Versus Goliath: Marbury Strikes Back

Marbury was incensed, and he turned to the courts for help. He sued the iconic James Madison, Jefferson's secretary of state (the government official in technical possession of the commission), seeking an order requiring that the commission be delivered to him. Jefferson was not pleased.

Marbury filed his lawsuit against Madison directly in the Supreme Court. Normally, a lawsuit would have to wend its way through the lower courts before the Supreme Court would even think about considering it, but Congress had passed a statute, the Judiciary Act of 1789, that allowed suits like the one brought by Marbury to bypass the lower courts and proceed in this rather unusual way.

Chief Justice Marshall felt that Marbury had been wronged by Jefferson, but he also felt that the Judiciary Act of 1789 violated the Constitution. Marshall's view was that the Constitution did not permit lawsuits like Marbury's to be filed in the Supreme Court, and he believed that Congress had overstepped its authority by enacting a statute that contradicted the Constitution's plain language.

Marshall's Masterstroke

Marbury's lawsuit presented on a silver platter the issue that Chief Justice Marshall longed to decide: whether the judiciary had the power to declare unconstitutional and therefore invalidate a law, in this case the Judiciary Act of 1789, that had been passed by a duly elected legislature and signed by a duly elected president, each of which comprises an equal branch of government. How could the three branches of government be equal if, in fact, one could effectively negate the actions of the other? Or, as Marshall put it through superlative understatement,

"The question, whether an act, repugnant to the constitution, can become the law of the land, is a question deeply interesting to the United States."

At the same time, Marshall realized that he was not merely deciding an important legal issue—he was defining the shape of the American system of government for succeeding generations. He knew that if he found in favor of Marbury and ordered Jefferson to issue the writ, Jefferson would likely ignore the order. He also knew that if he denied Marbury's claim, it would appear that the Court had kowtowed to the president. Either way, Marshall knew that, depending on what he did, the Court could be forever relegated to second-class status. And, knowing his legacy rested in the balance, Marshall was not about to allow that to happen.

Marshall, as adept at politics as he was at law, crafted a solution that, to this day, is recognized as a consummate judicial tour de force.

Initially, Marshall declared that Marbury should have received his commission, chastising Jefferson and avoiding the appearance of judicial subservience.

Marshall then ruled unconstitutional the act of Congress, the Judiciary Act of 1789, that gave the Supreme Court the power to hear Marbury's case and reverse what Jefferson had done. Bad news for Marbury; but in so doing, Marshall dodged a confrontation with Jefferson and simultaneously gave himself the opportunity to establish, once and for all, the right of the Supreme Court to void any law that the Supreme Court deemed, in its sole judgment, to violate the Constitution. Marshall capitalized on that opportunity, using logic and language that has resonated throughout our history.

Marshall wrote that the American people had a right to "establish, for their future government, such principles as, in their opinion, shall most conduce to their own happiness," and had done so in the form of a written Constitution. The Constitution represents the "original and supreme will" of the people and "is the basis on which the whole American fabric has been erected." From this, Marshall's ultimate conclusion, on which so much of America as it exists today is founded, logically followed:

"Certainly all those who have framed written constitutions contemplate them as forming the fundamental and paramount law of the nation, and consequently the theory of every such government must be that an act of the legislature repugnant to the constitution is void."

The Legacy of *Marbury v. Madison*

Consider where we might be had Chief Justice Marshall not taken this judicial leap of faith. Without *Marbury v. Madison* and the principles it entrenched, Congress, or a state legislature, or a local borough council would only be restrained by the fear of losing the next election. So long as the majority of voters remained either in favor of or apathetic about what government did, government officials could pass laws designed to eliminate free speech among their critics, arbitrarily restrict the use of private property, favor their race or religion over others, gerrymander election districts to effectively fix elections, and so on. In essence, they could do whatever they wanted, for so long as they could successfully manipulate the political process and stay in office.

But after *Marbury v. Madison* the rule book changed, and the players had to change along with it: Now, government officials know that at any time, a single citizen armed with a creative lawyer can invoke the power of the judiciary to measure their laws and decisions against constitutional standards. Each citizen, through this right to invoke the overriding authority of the Constitution, can play a direct role in controlling government, instead of government controlling each citizen. *Marbury v. Madison* gave us the opportunity to remain the government of laws, not men, that is a prime hallmark of our greatness as a nation.

To this day, virtually all constitutional law courses begin with *Marbury v. Madison,* and constitutional democracies throughout the world revere the decision as the wellspring of the checks and balances that make a true and lasting democracy feasible.

2. Did the Supreme Court Trigger the Civil War?

Dred Scott v. Sandford (1857)

The infamous *Dred Scott v. Sandford* decision was the first case since *Marbury v. Madison*, decided more than fifty years earlier, in which the Supreme Court used the power of judicial review to declare an act of Congress unconstitutional. It had all the elements of a Hollywood thriller—human pathos, a burning national crisis, backroom deals, moral activists facing off against big business, ethical weakness at the highest levels of government, the rise of an unknown crusader into the pantheon of history. Everything, that is, except a happy ending. The *Dred Scott* case reinforced the role of the Supreme Court as the institution to which American society turns for the final and binding decisions on its most incendiary issues. It also serves as the exemplar of how much damage can be done when the power of judicial review goes awry.

At its core, in the *Dred Scott* decision the Supreme Court ruled that slaves and free blacks were not citizens worthy of constitutional protection, and could lawfully be claimed as property, even in states that had outlawed slavery. The decision placed a stamp of approval on slavery, put a match to an already-smoldering blood feud between North and South, and accelerated a chain of events that ultimately elected Abraham Lincoln and overwhelmed whatever opportunity there had been to avoid civil war.

This "self-inflicted wound" (as one future justice described the case) seriously diminished the prestige and power of the Court for at least a generation.

Dred Scott's Suit for Freedom

After the ratification of the Constitution (which purposely failed to confront the legalities of slavery), the bitter fight between pro-slavery and anti-slavery forces intensified. This eventually led, in 1820, to the Missouri Compromise: as part of the admission of Maine and Missouri as states, Congress provided that (with the exception of Missouri itself) slavery would be prohibited in the territories north of the line that formed Missouri's southern border.

Dred Scott was a Virginia slave who had been sold to an army physician, Dr. Emerson, who, sometime after 1820, took him north of the Missouri Compromise line (where slavery was unlawful), and then back to Missouri (where slavery was lawful). In prior cases, numerous courts had ruled—and it was generally accepted—that once a slave set foot on free soil, he was emancipated. In 1850, Scott, who had saved some money, tried to buy his freedom from Dr. Emerson's widow, who now owned Scott. Dr. Emerson's widow refused, and Scott brought suit in Missouri state court claiming that, having lived in the free territory, he was now a free man.

A jury found in Scott's favor, but the Missouri Supreme Court reversed, ruling that it was "a humiliating spectacle to see a court of a state confiscate the property of her own citizens by the command of a foreign law." In other words, Dred Scott was property, and a contrary law enacted by a Congress situated far away, in Washington, D.C., was a "foreign law" that need not be followed.

Dred Scott's attorney responded by dropping his claims in state court and filing a lawsuit in federal court. Scott's position was this: citizens can sue in federal court; Scott was a citizen by virtue of his journey to a free territory; and the Missouri Compromise, a federal law, should be enforced for his benefit.

Scott lost, and the Supreme Court accepted the appeal.

Scott's case crystallized the most combustible issues of the time. Is a freed black a "citizen" who is entitled to protection under the Constitution, or merely property to be bought and sold? Does the federal government have the constitutional power to tell the states what to do about slavery?

As the Supreme Court mulled over the issues, the country became embroiled in a hurricane of pro-slavery versus anti-slavery debate. As emotions rose, Stephen A. Douglas, a well-known Illinois senator and orator, introduced a bill in Congress that sought to invalidate the Missouri Compromise in Kansas and Nebraska so that those states could decide the slavery issue for themselves, free from federal interference. This further outraged the North, leading to the formation of a new party, the Republican Party, which passionately opposed the extension of slavery into the territories. Angry and concerned citizens in both the North and South gathered and argued on street corners and in town halls.

The Decision and Its Aftermath: North v. South

Chief Justice Roger Taney announced the Supreme Court's decision on March 6, 1857. Joined by six other justices, he wrote that blacks had been regarded as holding an inferior status when the Constitution was adopted, and were therefore not "citizens" entitled to sue in federal court. That ruling effectively put Dred Scott out of court, and there was no reason for the decision to go further. But Chief Justice Taney did not stop there.

Invoking the Court's judicial review powers, Chief Justice Taney went on to rule that Congress had exceeded its constitutional authority when it enacted the Missouri Compromise. As a result, Dred Scott could no longer argue that because he had been taken to a free territory he was therefore emancipated—the Missouri Compromise was invalid and without legal effect, and consequently the territory north of the Missouri Compromise line was no longer free. Moreover, said Chief Justice Taney, it would be unconstitutional to deem a slave a free man merely because the slave had been taken into free territory, since that would deprive the slave owner of his rightful property, the slave, without just compensation: the government could not take a man's farm or livestock without paying him, and neither could it take a man's slaves.

The upshot was that slaves were to remain slaves, and the federal government had been stripped of the authority to do much about it.

Even formerly apathetic Northerners took the decision as a virtual call to arms, swelling the ranks of the militant abolitionists. Horace Greeley, the famed journalist and politician, owned the most influential newspaper of the time, the *New York Tribune*, in which he wrote that the *Dred Scott* decision "is entitled to just so much moral weight as would be the judgment of a majority of those congregated in any Washington bar-room." At the same time, the South was empowered, and Southern politicians and newspapers trumpeted the decision as a validation of states' rights, in particular the right of any established or new state to decide whether slavery would be legal within its borders, no matter what the federal government said.

Cynics speculated that some of the Supreme Court justices had been influenced by politics. Before the decision was reached, President-elect Buchanan (who had won the November 1856 election, but was still awaiting his inauguration) made no secret of the fact that he opposed the Missouri Compromise and wanted it overturned. In recent years, historians have uncovered evidence of patently unethical communications in which Buchanan lobbied at least two of the justices to sign on to Taney's opinion.

Lincoln Enters the Controversy

A year after the *Dred Scott* decision was announced, Lincoln, then an unknown on the national stage, challenged Douglas, then a leading candidate for the Democratic presidential nomination, for Douglas's Illinois senate seat. Lincoln initiated his campaign with one of his most famous speeches. He stressed the injustice in the fact that, according to the *Dred Scott* decision, a slave could live in a free state and yet still be a slave. Said Lincoln: "A house divided against itself cannot stand. I believe this government cannot endure, permanently half slave and half free." In the months that followed, the candidates engaged in the famous Lincoln-Douglas debates, in which Lincoln repeatedly railed at the *Dred Scott* decision and at all those who agreed that blacks were not entitled to protection under the precepts of the Declaration of Independence and the Constitution.

Douglas sought a middle ground, and in the process alienated both Northern and Southern voters. In the 1860 presidential campaign, Douglas got the Democratic nomination, but Southerners bolted from the party and nominated their own pro-slavery ticket. The Whigs also nominated their own ticket; and, riding the crest of the notoriety he obtained after *Dred Scott*, the Republican Party nominated Lincoln. This four-party election fractionalized the electorate — Lincoln received a minority of the popular vote, but won the electoral vote and, ironically, was sworn in as president by Chief Justice Taney himself in 1861.

Lincoln immediately faced Northerners who believed the *Dred Scott* decision would lead to future Supreme Court cases in which Northern states would be forbidden from banning slavery within their borders (Lincoln himself had fanned those flames in the Lincoln–Douglas debates). At the same time, he was confronted by Southerners who celebrated the prospect of slave auctions on the Boston Commons.

The rest, as the saying goes, is history.

Ultimately, the Fourteenth Amendment, adopted in 1868, provided that slaves were fully entitled to citizenship and constitutional protections, effectively overruling the *Dred Scott* decision and launching it into ignominy. That did little good in reality, however, as the so-called Black Codes of the Southern states imposed second-class status, and much worse, on Southern blacks until the federal government enacted and began to enforce, sometimes through military actions, meaningful civil rights legislation in the 1960s.

The *Dred Scott* case is, even today, cited as the poster child for those who decry "judicial activism." During his confirmation hearing, Chief Justice Roberts was asked if he agreed with a statement President Lincoln made in his first inaugural address. Lincoln said that if vital questions affecting the people were irrevocably decided by the Supreme Court (as opposed to the other branches of government), "the people will have ceased to be their own rulers." Chief Justice Roberts responded as follows:

> Well, President Lincoln, of course, was referring to one of the, perhaps the most, egregious examples of judicial activism in our history, the *Dred Scott* case. In which the court went far beyond what was necessary to decide the case, and really I think historians would say that the Supreme Court tried to put itself in the position of resolving the dispute about the extension of slavery and resolving it in a particular way that it thought was best for the nation. And we saw what disastrous consequences flowed from that.

As important as the *Dred Scott* decision is in the context of the Civil War and our larger history, there is another aspect to the case that makes it of foundational significance to our constitutional democracy: Lincoln abided by it. Lincoln excoriated the decision as both wrong and dangerous—and yet in the Lincoln-Douglas debates he argued that, nevertheless, it was a decision of the Supreme Court, and it must be respected until the Supreme Court says otherwise.

"We think its [the Supreme Court's] decisions on Constitutional questions, when fully settled, should control, not only the particular cases decided, but the general policy of the country, subject to be disturbed only by amendments of the Constitution as provided in that instrument itself," Lincoln said. And leaving no doubt as to his view on the supremacy of Supreme Court decisions, he then continued. "More than this would be revolution. But we think the *Dred Scott* decision is erroneous. We know the court that made it, has often over-ruled its own decisions, and we shall do what we can to have it to over-rule this. We offer no resistance to it."

This closed the loop on *Marbury v. Madison*: No matter how difficult the circumstances, no matter how entrenched the personal disagreements, the United States was to be a government of laws, not men.

As for Dred Scott himself, in 1857, Dr. Emerson's widow remarried. Her new husband opposed slavery, and she returned Scott to his former owners, the Blow family, who gave Scott and his family their freedom. The next year, Dred Scott died of tuberculosis. His headstone at Calvary Cemetery in St. Louis now bears the following epitaph:

DRED SCOTT BORN ABOUT 1799 DIED SEPT. 17, 1858.

DRED SCOTT

SUBJECT OF THE DECISION OF THE SUPREME COURT OF THE UNITED STATES IN 1857, WHICH DENIED CITIZENSHIP TO THE NEGRO, VOIDED THE MISSOURI COMPROMISE ACT, AND BECAME ONE OF THE EVENTS THAT RESULTED IN THE CIVIL WAR.

CHAPTER 2

ONE NATION UNDER GOD?
MATTERS OF CHURCH AND STATE

*"A union of government and religion tends to
destroy government and degrade religion."*

—HUGO L. BLACK, SUPREME COURT JUSTICE, 1937–71

The phrase "separation of church and state" is engrained in the American vernacular—but, contrary to the common mythology, the phrase does not appear in the Constitution. Jefferson lobbied for, as he put it, "a wall of separation between church and state," but other Founding Fathers sought no more than a constitutional provision forbidding the government from enshrining a national religion. They wanted religious freedom, and feared the religious persecution that would result if government were permitted to endorse one religion over another.

When all was said and done, the framers of the Constitution inserted into the First Amendment a provision known as the "Establishment Clause," which, as now interpreted, effectively provides that government "shall make no law respecting an establishment of religion."

The disagreement over what those words mean has spurred an ongoing constitutional holy war in which the hostilities continue, while the battlegrounds change.

In this 1891 Thomas Nast cartoon from *Harper's Weekly,* a woman symbolizing Justice stands at the door of a building labeled "State" as soldiers block the steps to members of different religions.

3. The School Prayer Case: Religion in the Public Schools

Engel v. Vitale (1962)

Legal scholars have debated the meaning of the Establishment Clause for decades. The words themselves do not reflect the adoption of Jefferson's point of view: there is no mandate that all religion be removed from the public arena. Still, at what point does the government's acceptance of or involvement in religion become "an establishment of religion"?

After a history of confusing and contradictory decisions, the Supreme Court began to clarify the practical meaning and impact of the Establishment Clause in the school prayer cases that captured the attention of the nation in the early 1960s.

Does School Prayer "Establish" Religion?

In many schools throughout the country, students were routinely required to begin the day with the recitation of a prayer. In New York, the state Board of Regents composed what they believed was a nondenominational prayer: "Almighty God, we acknowledge our dependence upon Thee, and we beg Thy blessing upon us, our parents, our teachers and our Country." The Regents suggested, but did not mandate, that the prayer be recited by all students at the commencement of each school day.

Claiming that the Regents' actions violated the Establishment Clause, a group of parents filed a lawsuit, *Engel v. Vitale*, which worked its way through the court system and eventually was heard by the Supreme Court.

Facing extreme pressure on both sides of the issue, a clear majority of the Supreme Court agreed that the Regents had overstepped their constitutional boundaries. Justice Black, writing for the majority, put the issue into its historical context, recalling "that this very practice of establishing governmentally composed prayers for religious services was one of the reasons which caused many of our early colonists to leave England and seek religious freedom in America." Justice Black reasoned that a prayer is by its very nature religious, and that "we think that the constitutional prohibition against laws respecting an establishment of religion must at least mean that in this country, it is no part of the business of government to compose official prayers for any group of the American people to recite as a part of a religious program carried on by government."

New York (and the many other states that supported its position) argued that the prayer could not constitute the establishment of religion because it was voluntary, and did not reference any particular faith. Justice Black was unpersuaded. The prayer, he reasoned, promotes religion, and that is enough, even if it is not coercive. And the fact that the prayer referred to no particular religion is inconsequential, since it still promotes a family of religions—those that believe in "Almighty God."

The Court's ultimate ruling was plainly stated: "We think that by using its public school system to encourage recitation of the Regents' prayer, the State of New York has adopted a practice wholly inconsistent with the Establishment Clause."

The rationale of *Engel v. Vitale*, handed down in 1962, was expanded and clarified the next year in the case of *Abington Township School District v. Schempp*, which declared the practice of school-sponsored Bible reading and the recitation of the Lord's Prayer to be similarly unconstitutional. The *Schempp* case is doubly significant. In it, the Supreme Court also laid down what is known as the "secular purpose" and "primary effect" tests for Establishment Clause cases: if either the purpose or the effect of a law or government action is to advance or inhibit religion, the Establishment Clause is implicated. Using these criteria, as well as similar criteria that evolved in subsequent Establishment Clause cases, the Supreme Court has ruled unconstitutional all manner of school-sponsored or school-endorsed prayers at graduation ceremonies and other school events.

The "Religion-Free Zone" Myth

The *Engel* and *Schempp* cases were the subject of much protest, and in the process their true meaning has become substantially distorted.

Neither case, as is so often stated, takes God out of the schools, or mandates that schools be "religion-free zones." *Engel* and *Schempp* in no way restrict the teaching of religion as a subject of academic study, and they do not prohibit individual students from saying a prayer, distributing religious literature, talking to students about their religious beliefs, forming Bible-study groups, or wearing religious clothing, subject to the same rules of orderly conduct and school administration as other, nonreligious behavior. The Supreme Court placed its focus on the role of government in promoting religion, not the role of students in practicing religion.

Even so, disagreements over the meaning of the Establishment Clause continue to abound. Many citizens (including several Supreme Court justices) stress that the framers of the Constitution were men who held not only an abiding belief in God, but also a belief that the nation itself owed its existence and future to God. Therefore, they argue, while the framers did indeed fear the establishment of a "state religion," they could not have intended to invalidate prayers and ceremonies that do no more than pay respect to God.

Engel and *Schempp* have been settled law for over forty years, and barring a dramatic shift in the makeup of the Court it is unlikely they will be overturned. On the school front, the Establishment Clause battleground has shifted from school ceremonies to school curriculum. The next battery of Supreme Court decisions in this area will likely define the difference between that which constitutes the teaching of science, ethics, or philosophy and that which constitutes the promotion and sponsorship of religion.

4. The *Scopes* "Monkey Trial" Revisited: The Teaching of Evolution, Creationism, and "Intelligent Design" in Public Schools

Epperson v. Arkansas (1968)

In the 1920s, fundamentalist religious groups lobbied public schools to prohibit the teaching of evolution, linking it with atheism. William Jennings Bryan, former secretary of state, three-time presidential candidate, famous orator, and staunch fundamentalist, personally championed this movement, labeling the teaching of evolution irrational and immoral. (As Bryan was fond of saying during his many orations, "It is better to trust in the Rock of Ages than to know the ages of rock.") Largely as a result of his efforts, in 1925 Tennessee passed a law, known as the Butler Act, which forbade the teaching in public schools of "any theory that denies the story of the Divine Creation of man as taught in the Bible, and to teach instead that man has descended from a lower order of animals."

The *Scopes* "Monkey Trial"

The ACLU immediately offered to defend anyone convicted under the Butler Act. Sensing an opportunity to bring publicity and commerce to their town, within a few months a group of businessmen in Dayton, Tennessee, persuaded a local biology teacher, John Scopes, to admit that he taught evolution and to invite prosecution as a test case. The prosecutors obliged.

Bryan immediately accepted an invitation to assist the prosecution. In response, Clarence Darrow, a staunch agnostic and one of the most famous lawyers and social crusaders of his day, volunteered to help the defense. The famous *Scopes* "Monkey Trial" was on.

The trial was covered by more than a hundred newspaper reporters from all parts of the country, as well as reporters from Europe. Twenty-two telegraphers sent out 165,000 words a day, and a Chicago radio station broadcast the trial nationally—the first live radio coverage of a criminal trial. Two movie cameramen had their film flown out daily from a specially prepared airstrip.

The defense originally challenged the Butler Act on Establishment Clause grounds, but Darrow took control, launched a frontal assault on Bryan himself, and called Bryan as a witness in the effort to get him to admit that whatever moral and religious teachings the Bible might provide, it was not "science" and could not be taken literally. Darrow's cross-examination of Bryan became the stuff of legend. Darrow took Bryan through the story of Jonah, accounts of the earth standing still, the story of creation as set forth in Genesis, whether Eve was actually created from Adam's rib, and so on. The exchanges between the two were blistering. Bryan accused Darrow of having no purpose other than "to cast ridicule on everybody who believes in the Bible." Darrow responded, "We have the purpose of preventing bigots and ignoramuses from controlling the education of the United States." (The play and movie *Inherit the Wind* dramatizes the trial, and the Darrow–Bryan confrontation in particular, but does so with much poetic license.)

Darrow knew that he could not possibly obtain an acquittal in the Dayton trial court—it was never contested that Scopes violated the Butler Act. He also knew that a challenge to the constitutionality of the Butler Act would be better pursued before an appeals court. Rather than trying to win the case in Dayton, Darrow's intent was to ridicule Bryan's position and turn public opinion against statutes like the Butler Act, and by many accounts he plainly succeeded. H. L. Mencken, a famous journalist who actually helped fund the defense, wrote that

Bryan was a "buffoon" and that his speeches were "theologic bilge," while characterizing the defense as "eloquent" and "magnificent." *Life* magazine awarded Bryan its "Brass Medal of the Fourth Class," writing that he had "successfully demonstrated by the alchemy of ignorance hot air may be transmuted into gold, and that the Bible is infallibly inspired except where it differs with him on the question of wine, women, and wealth."

Outfoxing Bryan, at the close of the trial Darrow literally told the judge to find Scopes guilty, and gave no final summation. Under Tennessee procedures, if Darrow gave no final summation, Bryan would be barred from making a final summation as well. Darrow knew that Bryan had been hungering to deliver a speech that Bryan later called "the mountain peak of my life's effort," a fire-and-brimstone, anti-evolution, fundamentalist oration for the assembled journalists and radio audience, and Darrow's tactic ended the trial before Bryan had his opportunity.

After nine minutes of deliberation, the jury found Scopes guilty, and the judge ordered him to pay a $100 fine (which Bryan offered to pay on Scopes's behalf). The defense appealed to the Tennessee Supreme Court. Among other arguments, the defense contended that the Butler Act violated the Establishment Clause, and was therefore unconstitutional. The Tennessee Supreme Court refused to so rule—but found an "out" and reversed the conviction anyway, ruling that under Tennessee law, the jury, not the judge, was to have decided the amount of the fine.

Having had enough, the prosecution never sought a retrial. The "Monkey Trial" remained part of American history and legend, but had no significant impact on American law for more than forty years. In the meantime, the anti-evolutionists vigorously continued their efforts, and laws similar to the Butler Act were enacted in Mississippi and Arkansas. The ACLU was unable to find another teacher willing to go through what Scopes had endured, and it was not until the 1960s, spurred by the

Supreme Court's Establishment Clause decisions in the school prayer cases, that the issue was again pursued, culminating in the Supreme Court's 1968 decision in *Epperson v. Arkansas.*

The *Scopes* "Monkey Trial" Redux

Arkansas's anti-evolution statute, passed in 1928, was in practical effect identical to the Butler Act, making it a crime "to teach the theory or doctrine that mankind ascended or descended from a lower order of animals" or "to adopt or use in any such institution a textbook" that holds this view. No one had ever been prosecuted under the law, but the Arkansas Education Association sought to challenge it on Establishment Clause grounds and, ultimately, it persuaded a high school teacher, Susan Epperson, to do so. The Arkansas Education Association brought a lawsuit in her name, seeking to have the law invalidated.

After a one-day trial, an Arkansas trial court judge ruled that the Arkansas law was unconstitutional, but the Arkansas attorney general appealed, and the Arkansas Supreme Court then reinstated the law as "a valid exercise of the state's power to specify the curriculum in its public schools." The Supreme Court accepted the appeal in order to finally settle the issue the *Scopes* "Monkey Trial" had raised but not resolved: whether states could ban the teaching of evolution in public schools, or whether such a ban was unconstitutional.

The result: A unanimous Supreme Court ruled that a ban on the teaching of evolution violates the Establishment Clause.

Justice Abraham Fortas, writing for the majority, explained that the Establishment Clause mandates that government maintain a position of neutrality in religious matters. "Government in our democracy, state and national, must be neutral in matters of religious theory, doctrine, and practice. It may not be hostile to any religion or to the advocacy of no-religion; and it may not aid, foster, or promote one religion or religious theory against another." Contrary to this tenet of law, the Court found that the sole reason for the Arkansas law was that a particular religious group considered the theory of evolution to be in conflict with the Bible's account of creation, a view that group favored. As a result, the Court ruled that "Arkansas's law cannot be defended as an act of religious neutrality."

The Evolution of the Creationists

Creationists responded with a switch in tactics. Rather than outlawing the teaching of evolution altogether, they successfully passed "equal time" or "balanced treatment" statutes that mandated that both evolution and "creation science" be taught. The rationale for these laws, went the argument, was that the teaching of various scientific theories would advance the cause of science instruction generally, which was a secular, nonreligious purpose beyond the reach of the Establishment Clause.

These efforts eventually found their way to the Supreme Court, in the 1987 decision in *Edwards v. Aguillard*, which directly confronted the issue of whether "creation science" was really science, or religion in scientific clothing. Seventy-two Nobel Prize–winning scientists, seventeen state academies of science, and seven other scientific organizations urged that "creation science" was, in fact, religion.

By a 7–2 majority, the Supreme Court agreed. The Court found that "the term 'creation science' . . . embodies the religious belief that a supernatural creator was responsible for the creation of humankind." This, said the Court, documented that "creation science" had as its primary purpose the advancement of a particular religious viewpoint— that is, the belief in a supreme being—and was therefore at odds with the Establishment Clause.

The *Edwards* decision, however, was equally unsuccessful in ending these confrontations. After *Edwards*, opponents of the teaching of evolution promoted the concept of "intelligent design" as a curriculum that could be taught in the public schools without offending the Establishment Clause. "Intelligent design" points to gaps in the theory of evolution, contends that nature exhibits a "purposeful arrangement of parts," and posits that an "intelligent designer" must therefore have been involved in creation generally and mankind in particular— but does not go so far as to state directly that the "intelligent designer" must be God.

Efforts to introduce this strain of intelligent design into public school curricula have consistently failed Establishment Clause challenges, but as the makeup of the Court changes, the question of where the Establishment Clause line is properly drawn will remain in flux, and the proponents and opponents of some form of an intelligent design curriculum may well find their way to the Supreme Court, where yet another chapter of the book that began with the *Scopes* "Monkey Trial" will be written.

5. Religion in Town Squares and Town Meetings

Van Orden v. Perry (2005)
McCreary County, Kentucky v. ACLU of Kentucky (2005)
Town of Greece v. Galloway (2014)

The school prayer and creationism cases provided substantial clarity to the dispute over religion in the public schools: government is not supposed to endorse one religion or religious viewpoint over another, implicitly or explicitly. But how does this principle play out in other aspects of federal, state, and local government? Can tax dollars be lawfully spent on religious monuments? Do legislatures and town councils violate their obligations of religious neutrality when they begin their sessions with Christian prayers?

The Ten Commandments Cases

In two related Supreme Court cases decided in 2005, *Van Orden v. Perry* and *McCreary County, Kentucky v. ACLU of Kentucky*, the Supreme Court determined whether state-sponsored displays of the Ten Commandments on public property violate the Establishment Clause. The *Van Orden* case arose when, approximately fifty years ago, a patriotic organization presented Texas with a six-foot monolith inscribed with the Ten Commandments. Texas chose to display the monument on state land at state expense, between the Texas State Capitol and the Texas Supreme Court, among approximately twenty other monuments of varying types and themes. The *McCreary* case is based on more recent events. Two Kentucky counties posted large, highly visible copies of the Ten Commandments in their courthouses.

Both displays were challenged in court: The issue was whether displaying the Ten Commandments on public property brought church and state too close together, in violation of the Establishment Clause. The Supreme Court, seeking an opportunity to clarify how separate church and state must be, agreed to hear the appeals of these cases.

By a 5–4 margin, the Court ruled that some intermixture between church and state is permissible, and that the Texas display did not violate the Establishment Clause. However, the Court also ruled that too much intermixture is impermissible, and that the Kentucky display did violate the Establishment Clause. Where is the line, and how does one find it?

To resolve these issues, the *McCreary* and *Van Orden* cases relied on a sometimes-discredited 1971 Supreme Court decision, *Lemon v. Kurtzman*, which gave birth to what is known in constitutional law circles as the "*Lemon* test." According to the *Lemon* test, in order to satisfy the Establishment Clause, government conduct must have a secular purpose, it must have a primary effect that neither advances nor inhibits religion, and it must not foster excessive government entanglement with religion. In most contexts, the *Lemon* test asks judges to determine if the *real* purpose and effect of a government action trends more toward the religious or more toward the secular.

The Texas Ten Commandments monument was part of a larger display that highlighted the role of both religious and secular influences in law, government, and history. Admittedly, the Ten Commandments is a religious icon; but, to the majority of the justices, the purpose and effect of the Texas Ten Commandments display was not primarily religious, in the sense of extolling the Ten Commandments for its spiritual content, but rather it focused on the historical and cultural role of the Ten Commandments in a larger, nonreligious context. The 5–4 majority allowed the Texas monument to stand for these reasons.

But the same could not be said about the Kentucky display. The Ten Commandments display was put there by itself, within no larger historic or cultural context, and for no apparent purpose other than to endorse the Ten Commandments for its own sake. Because there was no independent, secular reason to justify the display of a religious symbol, the 5–4 majority required that the Kentucky display be removed.

Can You Begin a Public Meeting with a Christian Prayer?

In 1999, Greece, a town in upstate New York, began inviting local members of the clergy to lead prayer sessions to open town board meetings. Members of the public attended the meetings to debate zoning applications, address local issues and, generally, to participate in local government. Almost always, the participating clergy members were Christian, and the content of the prayers included distinctly Christian content and themes, invoking "Jesus," "Christ," "Your Son," or "the Holy Spirit." The town never denied any clergy the opportunity to give a prayer, but it did not publicize this open-door policy.

In 2010, two local residents brought suit, claiming that the prayer practice violated the Establishment Clause—that is, the prayer practice had the effect of establishing religion.

Town of Greece v. Galloway was decided by the Supreme Court in 2014. In the nine-year interim between the *Van Orden* and *McCreary* cases and the *Town of Greece* case, Justices Rehnquist, Stevens, O'Connor, and Souter had been replaced by Justices Roberts, Alito, Sotomayor, and Kagan, and the four-member "conservative" and "liberal" voting blocs had coalesced.

Predictably, the conservative bloc and Justice Kennedy voted to allow the prayers to continue, and the liberal bloc strongly dissented. But what was not so predictable was the basis for these competing points of view: other than in a brief aside, *neither* the majority nor the minority even mentioned the *Lemon* case, the case that had been the starting point for Establishment Clause cases for decades. Rather, Justice Kennedy, who wrote the majority opinion, and Justice Kagan, who wrote the primary dissenting opinion, disagreed over history.

Justice Kennedy claimed that prayers at public meetings were endorsed by the framers, and were "meant to lend gravity to the occasion and reflect values long part of the nation's heritage." They were permissible, he wrote, so long as other religions were not denigrated and no one was required to participate in the prayers.

Justice Kagan cited evidence that while the framers did not ban prayer in public meetings, they did insist on neutrality. Opening prayers must be "inclusive of different faiths, rather than always identified with a single religion." The Town of Greece prayers, she wrote, "put some residents to the unenviable choice of either pretending to pray like the majority or declining to join its communal activity, at the very moment of petitioning their elected leaders."

How Much Religion Is Too Much Religion?

What do the *Van Orden*, *McCreary*, and *Town of Greece* decisions bode for the future of church–state relationships?

The fact that the Supreme Court will not mandate anything approaching a total "separation of church and state" was a foregone conclusion; after all, as has been the tradition for many years, every Supreme Court session begins with a Supreme Court official intoning "God save the United States and this Honorable Court," and it is not likely that the "In God We Trust" inscription will be removed from the money supply any time soon.

Judicial conservatives have for many years believed that the *Lemon* test unlawfully restricts the role of religion in American life, and they have argued, often passionately, for its elimination from our church–state jurisprudence. Justice Scalia has written (as only he could) that, implicitly if not explicitly, prior Supreme Court decisions had already overruled the *Lemon* test and, yet, it continues to live, like "some ghoul in a late-night horror movie that repeatedly sits up in its grave and shuffles abroad, after repeatedly being killed and buried." *McCreary* and *Van Orden* seemed to establish that, as the saying goes, the rumors of the *Lemon* test's demise have been greatly exaggerated.

And then came the *Town of Greece* decision, where the *Lemon* test was extremely conspicuous by its absence. The law had not changed. Rather, the Court had changed, and the *Town of Greece* decision was made by a *much* different Court than the one that decided *Van Orden* and *McCreary*.

The *Town of Greece* decision continues the trend of ignoring the *Lemon* test when it gets in the way of the justices' view of where the line should be drawn between majority and minority religious views and expressions and, moreover, it sheds substantial light on where the current Roberts Court stands after the passing of Justice Scalia: four justices believe that it is not the role of the Court to involve itself in protecting minority religions from the majority's expression of its religious beliefs, so long as the minority is not otherwise denigrated or prejudiced; four of the justices believe that while the Establishment Clause does not erect a wall between church and state, it does mandate that the Court enforce religious neutrality in government and public institutions.

What happens next? That will depend on *who* happens next. If the past proves anything, it proves that in matters of church and state, each future Supreme Court justice's experience and values will influence how precedent is interpreted and applied. There is a human element that cannot be removed from these equations. As the roster of justices changes, so will the legal precepts that guide our way.

6. Can a Religious Belief Negate a Legal Requirement?

Burwell v. Hobby Lobby Stores, Inc. (2014)

Suppose Congress (or a state, or a city—or a township, for that matter) considers a proposed law, holds hearings, debates it thoroughly, and passes it. Should people be permitted to violate the law—a law that others must respect—based on their religious beliefs? What about the concept of equal justice under law?

For instance, consider laws that require parents to send their children to approved public or private schools, or to homeschool them in accordance with state-mandated criteria. You may object to these requirements because you think they are irrational and counterproductive, but you still have to abide by them. But suppose your neighbor asserts his First Amendment rights, and objects to educating his children on certain subjects based on his religious beliefs—does he get to violate those laws, just because his objections are religion-based, and yours are not?

Let's make the problem even more difficult. Many laws are written to foster the common good—a common good that could be torpedoed if some people refuse to comply. For instance, suppose your community enacts a noise ordinance—no loud music between 10 P.M. and 7 A.M. What if the people down the street subscribe to a religion that mandates religious services, including loud music and song, every sunrise?

Or suppose a school district enacts an ordinance requiring the vaccination of all school children against a virus that has sickened many people in an adjoining town. What if one family claims that medical interventions violate their religious beliefs, and they assert their First Amendment right to refuse to have their six children vaccinated? Do different laws apply to different people based on their religious beliefs? Is religion a "get out of jail free" card?

Let's make this even more difficult. Suppose a profit-making corporation claims that it has the right to break a law that specifically applies to all corporations—a law that its competition has to respect—because of the religious beliefs of the people who own the corporation. Does a corporation have the right to claim legal exemptions based on religion?

Welcome to the conundrums that led to the Supreme Court's 2014 decision in *Burwell v. Hobby Lobby Stores, Inc.* Not surprisingly, it was another Roberts Court 5–4 decision, with all of the so-called liberal/Democratic justices on one side, all of the so-called conservative/Republican justices on the other side, and Justice Kennedy left with the deciding vote. This time, Justice Kennedy allied with the conservative wing, tilting the balance in that direction. Justice Alito wrote the majority opinion, and Justice Ginsburg wrote a passionate dissent.

How the Case Arose

In 2010, Congress passed the Patient Protection and Affordable Care Act, colloquially known as "Obamacare" and referred to here as the "ACA." As authorized by the ACA, the Department of Health and Human Services (HHS) issued regulations requiring certain employers' group health plans to provide women with coverage for twenty types of contraceptive methods approved by the Food and Drug Administration, without any cost-sharing requirements.

Hobby Lobby Stores, Inc. is an arts and crafts company with approximately 21,000 employees. It was founded by David Green, a self-made billionaire. Conestoga Wood Specialties is a furniture company owned by the Hahn family, who are Mennonites, and it has about 1,000 employees.

In 2012, Hobby Lobby, Conestoga Wood, and another company owned by a member of the Green family (for shorthand purposes, the "*Hobby Lobby* plaintiffs") filed a lawsuit claiming that while most of the FDA-approved contraceptive methods prevent the fertilization of an egg, four of the contraceptive methods might have the effect of preventing an already fertilized egg from developing any further by inhibiting its attachment to the uterus. This, the *Hobby Lobby* plaintiffs asserted, was the equivalent of abortion, and it violated the religious beliefs of the owners of the companies. On that basis the *Hobby Lobby* plaintiffs sought an injunction exempting them from the ACA's requirement that they fund insurance coverage that would make these contraceptive methods available to their employees.

The law on which the case would be decided was enacted in 1993. Seeking to nullify a prior Supreme Court decision that, in confrontations between law and religion, gave the benefit of the doubt to the law, Congress enacted the Religious Freedom Restoration Act (RFRA). RFRA mandated that once someone can show that a law significantly burdens their religious beliefs, then the law will be deemed invalid unless the government can prove, first, that the law serves an extremely important purpose and, second, that there is no other, less burdensome way to serve that purpose.

The Supreme Court had to determine how, consistent with the Constitution, RFRA applied to the *Hobby Lobby* plaintiffs' contention that they should not be required, like other companies, to provide the disputed contraception coverage to their employees.

The Majority's Decision

Justice Alito, writing for the majority, first had to decide whether business corporations, like Hobby Lobby and Conestoga Wood, could assert rights of religious freedom. This was, and remains, a substantial point of contention. Obviously, corporations, not being people, do not have religious beliefs. And in the eyes of the law, corporations are treated as something separate from the people who own them—corporations own their own assets, have their own liabilities, pay their own taxes, contract in their own name, all separately from their owners.

Justice Alito found that these corporations—the *Hobby Lobby* plaintiffs—could assert religious rights because, even though they were very sizeable businesses, they were each privately owned by family members, and in that sense they were more like small groups of people that had joined together to pursue a common purpose. Justice Alito left for another day the question of whether large, publicly owned companies could assert similar rights. (His decision reinforces a similar, controversial ruling in the *Citizens United* case.)

Having cleared that hurdle, Justice Alito analyzed how RFRA applied to the *Hobby Lobby* facts. Under RFRA, the first question was whether the contraception regulations, if violated, would seriously burden the *Hobby Lobby* plaintiffs and, therefore, the religious beliefs of its owners. Justice Alito had little difficulty with that issue—the penalties for a violation could be huge, even hundreds of millions of dollars per year.

The question then became whether the government had established that there was no less burdensome way—an alternative other than requiring the *Hobby Lobby* plaintiffs to comply with the regulations—to provide the *Hobby Lobby* plaintiffs' employees with the mandated coverage for the four challenged contraceptive methods.

Justice Alito concluded that there was a less burdensome alternative: He turned to the solution the Obama administration had devised for religious organizations, such as churches. In those instances, the religious organization can certify its objection to its insurance company, which will then issue a separate contraceptive policy to the organization's female employees—and the government, not the orga-nization, will pay the cost of the policy. (The Supreme Court later agreed to hear a challenge to that solution as well. Given the majority's seeming endorsement of this approach in *Hobby Lobby*, it seemed unlikely that the Court would overturn it. The case, *Zubik v. Burwell*, reached the Supreme Court after Justice Scalia's death and while the Senate was refusing to consider President Obama's proposed appoint-ment. In May 2016, after hearing argument and after requesting sup-plemental briefs from the parties, the Court, in a very unusual move, refused to decide the case, most likely because the vote was four-to-four and the Court did not want to underline the fact that the political process had rendered it unable to decide close cases.)

The result: The *Hobby Lobby* plaintiffs were exempted from complying with the regulations based on the religious beliefs of its owners.

Justice Ginsburg's Dissent

Justice Ginsburg angrily disagreed. She called the majority opinion a "decision of startling breadth" through which profit-making businesses could simply cite their owners' religious beliefs, and through that means determine which laws they will and will not be required to follow. This, she said, elevated the owners' religious beliefs over the disadvantages that their religion-based opt-outs impose on others—a company could raise a religious objection to virtually anything, and "the government, i.e., the general public, can pick up the tab."

Further, Justice Ginsburg argued that the majority opinion also elevated the rights of a corporation's owners over the rights of the cor-poration's employees. She referenced an oft-invoked maxim in free-speech cases: "Your right to swing your arms ends just where the other man's nose begins." There was no basis to favor the religious choices of corporate owners over the rights of their employees, she contended, as if religion provided a carte blanche exemption, despite the consequences suffered by others.

Finally, Justice Ginsburg was concerned about the possibility that, in endorsing the primacy of a religious objection over a law by which all others were bound, the majority had opened a door to employers who, on various religious bases, would object to a variety of medical treatments, the use of intravenous fluids, medicines derived from certain animals, pills coated with certain substances, and so on. In view of the *Hobby Lobby* decision, she argued, could the Supreme Court fail to accord equal status to the varied religious objections likely to be raised by Christian Scientists, Jehovah's Witnesses, Hindus, and a host of other religious belief systems?

Justice Alito stressed that the majority opinion only applied to contraception, and in a concurring opinion Justice Kennedy, seeking to assure Justice Ginsburg, offered his view that the majority opinion was narrowly focused. Justice Ginsburg disagreed. The majority, she wrote, has "ventured into a minefield."

Will the *Hobby Lobby* Door Open or Close in the Future?

The critics of *Hobby Lobby* focus not only on the specific result it reached, but also on the door its rationale may have opened, well beyond the health-care context. They argue that if, based on the religious beliefs of its owners, the *Hobby Lobby* plaintiffs could dictate what health plans they offered, then other private companies, based on a variety of other religious beliefs of their owners, could refuse to provide equal pay to men and women, hire only employees who subscribed to certain religious views, oppose the rights of minorities, mandate employee contributions to religious institutions . . . the list goes on, all connected by the common fear that *Hobby Lobby* will accord religious beliefs an expansive primacy over legal rights.

Many Supreme Court cases are criticized for opening a dangerous door, and over time these fears often prove to be alarmist and unwarranted extrapolations. But, sometimes, the fears are borne out by future decisions.

In their opinions, Justice Alito and Justice Kennedy predict that the *Hobby Lobby* decision will not be expansively applied in other contexts. But whether or not that turns out to be true will depend not on Justice Alito or Justice Kennedy as much as it will depend on the future appointments to the Court, and neither Justice Alito nor Justice Kennedy, nor anyone else, can predict who those future appointees will be, and how they may, or may not, use the *Hobby Lobby* decision as a launchpad for future rulings.

CHAPTER 3

INNOCENT UNTIL PROVEN GUILTY: THE RIGHTS OF THE ACCUSED

*"Better that ten guilty persons escape
than that one innocent suffer."*

—WILLIAM BLACKSTONE, EIGHTEENTH-CENTURY ENGLISH JURIST

Our Founding Fathers were mindful of the penchant of monarchs to charge persons with false crimes as a means of political oppression and social control. Consequently, they built copious protections for those accused of criminal offenses into the foundations of the Constitution. It was acknowledged that giving all benefits of the doubt to the accused would result in some guilty persons being set free, and yet they freely accepted this necessary evil as a price of freedom.

The story is told of a Chinese law professor who was advised of our belief that it was better that a thousand guilty men go free than one innocent man be executed.

The Chinese professor thought for a bit and asked, "Better for whom?"

The Founding Fathers' answer to that question was this: Better for all, because as history has proven, if anyone can be unlawfully jailed, everyone can be unlawfully jailed.

A witness stand in the Plymouth, Massachusetts, County Courthouse, 1966.

7. The Right to Be Represented by Counsel When Charged with a Crime

Gideon v. Wainwright (1963)

The Sixth Amendment to the Constitution provides that in criminal prosecutions, the accused has the right "to have the Assistance of Counsel for his defence." Based on this constitutional mandate, federal courts have for many years appointed lawyers for criminal defendants who are without the means to hire a lawyer on their own. However, until the 1960s, the law was unclear as to whether the Sixth Amendment also applied to the states, where the vast majority of criminal prosecutions took place. As a result, the Supreme Court left it to each state to decide for itself whether indigent defendants charged in state courts would be provided with lawyers—and this resulted in innumerable unrepresented people being convicted of crimes they claimed they had not committed.

In 1961, Clarence Gideon was accused of robbing a pool hall in Florida, and was charged with various crimes in a Florida state court. Gideon could not afford a lawyer, and at his trial he asked the judge to appoint a lawyer for him so that, as promised by the Sixth Amendment, he could have the assistance of counsel. The judge refused, in compliance with Florida law at the time, and Gideon was left to defend himself. Gideon maintained that he was innocent but, unschooled in the law, he did not do a good job defending himself at his trial. He was convicted and sentenced to five years in jail.

Gideon's Trumpet

From his jail cell, Gideon wrote out a petition to the Supreme Court of the United States. Gideon's position was simply this: An individual's ability to exercise his constitutional rights, in this case his Sixth Amendment right to have the assistance of counsel, should not depend on his wealth, or anything else. All Americans should have the same constitutional rights, in theory and in practice.

The Supreme Court agreed to hear Gideon's appeal. At the root of the case was this issue: Could a defendant in a criminal case conceivably get a fair trial without the assistance of a lawyer?

In its decision, the Supreme Court detailed the extent to which our courts are subject to specialized procedures and rules, and the fact that the knowledge and skill required to assemble and conduct a defense take years of training and experience to acquire. As a result, the Court reasoned, "The right to be heard would be, in many cases, of little avail if it did not comprehend the right to be heard by counsel." Without counsel, the Court concluded, an innocent defendant "faces the danger of conviction because he does not know how to establish his innocence."

On these bases, the Supreme Court invalidated Gideon's conviction, ordered a retrial, and required that a lawyer be appointed to defend him. At his new trial, with the help of a lawyer, Gideon was acquitted of the crime.

Fifty years ago, it was routine for indigent persons to be charged with crimes and forced to defend themselves in state courts without the assistance of a lawyer; that scenario is now constitutionally unimaginable. Clarence Gideon changed the law, inspiring the book and movie *Gideon's Trumpet* (with Henry Fonda playing Gideon). As Robert F. Kennedy put it, "If an obscure Florida convict named Clarence Earl Gideon had not sat down in his prison cell . . . to write a letter to the Supreme Court . . . the vast machinery of American law would have gone on functioning undisturbed. But Gideon did write that letter, the Court did look into his case . . . and the whole course of American legal history has been changed."

8. "You Have the Right to Remain Silent . . .": The Privilege Against Self-Incrimination

Miranda v. Arizona (1966)

Consider this situation: A kidnapping and sexual assault occurs. The police arrest a suspect and take him to the police station, where he is identified by the victim. In accordance with standard operating procedures, the suspect is then taken into a private interrogation room. The suspect is not advised that he has the right to be represented by a lawyer before he is questioned. Two hours later, the suspect signs a confession. There is no evidence that the suspect was physically or mentally abused in any way. The confession includes a statement that the suspect has "full knowledge of my legal rights, understanding any statement I make may be used against me," and that he had knowingly waived those rights. The suspect is put on trial, the confession is read to the jury, and the suspect is convicted.

Anything wrong with that?

These are the basic facts in the famous *Miranda* case, decided in 1966, in which the Supreme Court, in a 5–4 decision, ruled that once Ernesto Miranda was taken into police custody and before any interrogation could begin, the police had the constitutional duty under the Fifth Amendment to advise him that he had the right to refuse to answer any questions and to be represented by a lawyer, and if Miranda chose to take advantage of those rights, the police could not interrogate him in any way. Because the police failed to advise Miranda of these rights—now known as "Miranda rights"—before they questioned him and obtained his confession, Miranda's conviction was thrown out, just as innumerable convictions since the *Miranda* decision have been thrown out for similar reasons.

Taking the Fifth

The Fifth Amendment to the Constitution commands that no person "shall be compelled in any criminal case to be a witness against himself." As fundamental as this right is, however, it has an image problem. The Fifth Amendment is popularly viewed as a "legal technicality"—a loophole guilty people can use in their effort to beat the system. In television and movies, street-savvy punks and sophisticated white-collar criminals smugly refuse to answer questions in the police station, while they mock the detectives' impotence. The evening news televises congressional hearings in which reputed organized-crime figures and alleged corporate looters mechanically recite, "I assert my Fifth Amendment right against self-incrimination."

But the Fifth Amendment is anything but a legal technicality or a loophole.

It is easier and quicker for law-enforcement authorities to solve a crime by coercing a confession than it is to solve a crime through tedious investigation, particularly where the evidence may be hard to come by. In the seventeenth century, this fact of life led to horrific injustices in England (and elsewhere), in which innocent people were jailed on the basis of confessions made only after physical abuse or threats of harm. In reaction (some say revolution) against these wrongs, the right against self-incrimination—that is, the right to make law enforcement prove its case without the testimony of the suspect—became entrenched as a bedrock principle of English law. The Founding Fathers brought this precept with them to the colonies. They knew the horrors of the Old World too well and resolved to build the right against self-incrimination into the framework of the Constitution.

Still, the issue the Supreme Court faced in *Miranda* was different. By the time the *Miranda* case arose, it was a given that the police could not coerce a suspect to confess and then use that confession against him.

And even Miranda's lawyers did not argue that anyone had coerced a confession out of him: He was put into an interrogation room, confronted by the police, and after a couple of hours of questioning, he signed a statement.

Ignorance of the Law Can Be an Excuse

The Supreme Court ruled that this was not enough to protect Miranda's Fifth Amendment rights. It reviewed the many studies showing how subtle, psychological techniques can be used to intimidate unsophisticated suspects into signing an untrue confession. The Fifth Amendment, said the Court, prohibits much more than beatings with rubber hoses and the "third degree."

More important, the Supreme Court ruled that the Fifth Amendment is so crucial that law-enforcement officials must make certain that a suspect is aware of the right to remain silent and the right to counsel, before any questioning can take place—and the rule applies not only when the police seek to directly question a suspect, but also when they try to elicit incriminating evidence through intimidation or manipulation techniques. If the suspect then intelligently and voluntarily waives his rights, so be it, but you cannot waive a right until you know that the right exists, and it is up to law enforcement to make certain that persons in their custody have this knowledge. Otherwise, said the Court, the potential for abuse is far greater than is tolerable in a civilized society.

After *Miranda* was decided, television viewers and moviegoers were routinely treated to chase scenes in which sprinting police officers tackle desperate criminals, at which time one of the officers triumphantly instructs an underling, "Read him his rights" ("You have the right to remain silent, anything you say can and will be used against you in a court of law . . .").

In this context, Miranda rights seem formulaic and silly, and it is easy to ignore their true significance. But the message of the case is of colossal importance: Every individual accused of a crime has the right and the power to require that the government prove its accusations through real, substantive evidence, and every individual is provided with safeguards, like a lawyer and an unbiased court, to fend off the ability of those in power to get you if they want to.

As for Ernesto Miranda himself, his confession was thrown out. The police assembled the evidence, retried him, and he was convicted.

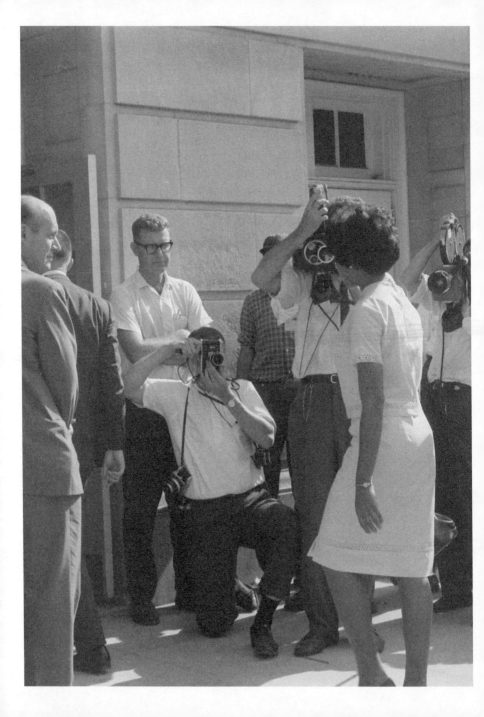

CHAPTER 4

THE MELTING POT: RACE, DISCRIMINATION, AND DIVERSITY

*"The one place where a man ought to get a square deal
is in a courtroom, be he any color of the rainbow . . ."*

—ATTICUS FINCH, IN *TO KILL A MOCKINGBIRD* BY HARPER LEE

I t has often been observed that the history of America is in many ways the history of race relations. The Supreme Court has written much of that history, often with regrettable results. Ultimately, however, the Court turned prior law on its head, declared racial segregation unconstitutional, and literally changed America. The resulting anti-discrimination inertia not only led to expanded rights for minorities; it also launched anti-discrimination efforts in many other contexts, such as gender, age, religion, nationality, and sexual orientation, to name a few.

But here's the complication. Where is the line between prohibiting discrimination against individuals based on, for instance, their race or nationality, and *favoring* individuals based on their race or nationality? Isn't that discrimination in reverse? And what about the right of people to be left alone? If they want to associate only with people of their own race, or gender, or sexual orientation, should the law be able to stop them?

Vivian Malone, one of the first African Americans to attend the University of Alabama, walks through a crowd that includes photographers, National Guard members, and Deputy U.S. Attorney General Nicholas Katzenbach, June 11, 1963.

9. Separate Is Not Equal: The End of Legalized Segregation

Brown v. Board of Education (1954)

The aftermath of slavery plagued the twentieth century, as segregation remained a practical reality throughout much of the North, and was mandated by state and local laws throughout the South. Blacks attempted to challenge segregation in the courts, but in 1896, in the case of *Plessy v. Ferguson*, the Supreme Court openly endorsed the concept of "separate but equal." On the basis of that precedent, local courts, as well as the Supreme Court itself, repeatedly refused to rule that segregation in education (or anything else) was unconstitutional.

In the 1930s, the NAACP developed a legal strategy to challenge the "separate but equal" concept: in one school after another, it successfully showed that the separate educational facilities being provided to blacks were not equal, and were in fact vastly inferior. By the 1950s, however, the NAACP's legal team—led by Thurgood Marshall, later to serve as the Supreme Court's first black justice—concluded that it would take decades to effect real change by challenging segregation on a case-by-case basis. Instead, the decision was made to challenge the "separate but equal" doctrine of *Plessy v. Ferguson* head-on. *Brown v. Board of Education* was the result.

The NAACP lawyers' argument was simply this: segregated schools were inherently unequal and could not be made equal, and forcing blacks to attend such schools violated the constitutional guaranty of equal protection under law. The NAACP contended, through the testimony of social scientists, that segregation itself was the problem: no matter how good the buildings, teachers, and curriculum might be, segregation, by its very nature, diminished the self-esteem and educational development of black children.

The Supreme Court Rules . . .
and Society Changes

The case was argued in the Supreme Court for a remarkable six days (usually, each side is limited to about an hour), and in a unanimous opinion brokered through the arduous efforts of Chief Justice Warren, the Supreme Court adopted the NAACP's position. "Segregation of white and colored children in public schools has a detrimental effect upon the colored children," the chief justice wrote in the Court's opinion, and the detriment is even "greater when it has the sanction of law, for the policy of segregating the races is usually interpreted as denoting the inferiority of the Negro group." Overruling more than a half century of precedent, Warren plainly stated that the doctrine of "separate but equal" has no place in American education—and, by implication, anywhere else in America.

But, having so ruled, the Court was left to decide what to do about segregated schools. Chief Justice Warren felt that he could not set a timetable for desegregation, and instead ruled that children must be admitted to public schools without regard for their race "with all deliberate speed." That now-famous phrase led to hundreds of local court challenges to desegregation measures in both the North and South, and even the use of federal troops to enforce local court desegregation decisions. But after enduring one of the most explosively divisive episodes in American history, by the early 1970s almost half of all black children in the South attended predominantly white schools—a higher percentage of desegregation than existed in the North.

As significant as the desegregation of public schools has proven to be, the reach of *Brown v. Board of Education* extends much further. The case sparked a firestorm of protests while at the same time creating much of the impetus for the Civil Rights Act of 1964; it spurred a string of later decisions that eliminated the legal underpinnings for other aspects of segregation in American life; and it laid much of the groundwork for the civil rights movement that continues today. Many legal commentators consider *Brown v. Board of Education* to be the most significant Supreme Court decision of the twentieth century.

10. Can One Race or Nationality Be Favored over Another in the Name of Diversity?

Gratz v. Bollinger (2003)
Grutter v. Bollinger (2003)
Fisher v. University of Texas (2016)

Should Your Race Ever Matter?

In the 1990s, the University of Michigan utilized an admissions policy in its undergraduate school that assigned a predetermined number of points to various admissions criteria such as grades, standardized test scores, quality of high school, residence, legacy status, and so on: the higher the point total, the greater the chance that an applicant would be admitted. The university wished to increase the diversity of its student population in order to serve its educational objectives and, therefore, it also added points to an applicant's admissions score if the applicant was a member of certain minority or racial groups that were underrepresented on campus. As the system existed in 1999, applicants who were members of these minority or racial groups would receive twenty extra points. This was significant—applicants with at least one hundred points were automatically admitted.

At about the same time, the University of Michigan Law School also sought to achieve diversity in its student body. However, in its admission process, the law school did not use a points system. Rather, it considered the usual factors (grades, standardized tests, recommendations, and so on), and also a variety of subjective and nontraditional criteria, one of which being whether the applicant would increase diversity. The law school did not limit its diversity goals to race or ethnicity—it also sought, for instance, geographic and economic diversity—but it did admit that it actively sought a "critical mass" of minority students.

Two well-qualified white Michigan residents who were denied admission as undergraduates, and one well-qualified white Michigan resident who was denied admission to the law school, filed suit against the university's president, claiming that they had been discriminated against on the basis of their race in violation of the Constitution and the Civil Rights Act of 1964. Ultimately, in 2003, these related "reverse discrimination" cases ended up in the Supreme Court: *Gratz v. Bollinger* (dealing with the university's undergraduate admission policy), and *Grutter v. Bollinger* (dealing with the university's law-school admission policy).

The Supreme Court's Balancing Act

The issue involved the collision of two worthy goals. One goal was the avoidance of racism in any form. As a fundamental, bedrock principle, discrimination on the basis of race is unlawful. In America, we are to be judged by our qualifications, not our color. The other goal was diversification in our educational institutions. For all sorts of reasons, going as far back as *Brown v. Board of Education*, the Supreme Court agreed with the educators, sociologists, and other experts who concluded that "separate but equal" does not work, and diverse student bodies foster excellence in education.

But how can you increase diversity in a student body without considering the race of those you are considering for admission into that student body?

The Supreme Court justices were bitterly divided over how best to balance these competing goals. Rather than speaking in one voice, the vote was split, and even those justices who agreed on the result wrote separate opinions expressing different rationales. But out of this confusion, a portentous message emerged.

In the *Gratz* case, involving the University of Michigan undergraduate school, the Court found the admissions procedure to be unconstitutional by a 6–3 margin. Any consideration of race must be very narrowly tailored, the Court ruled, and automatically awarding points for minority status was analogous to a quota system and was over the line.

But in the *Grutter* case, involving the University of Michigan Law School, the Court ruled otherwise, although by only a 5–4 margin. It found that by reviewing each student individually (and less mechanically), and by crediting diversity factors aside from just race, the racial aspects of the admissions criteria had been sufficiently narrowed to satisfy constitutional requirements.

Is *Grutter* an Aberration? Or the Start of a New Approach to Race Relations?

In the *Grutter* case, a majority of the Court crossed what had been a virtually impenetrable racial divide: The Supreme Court ruled that, at least in the educational context, color blindness is no longer legally mandated in America, and that overt racial favoritism (the other side of which is racial discrimination) can be legal, in narrowly defined circumstances, when necessary to promote a compelling social interest—in this case, diversity in an educational institution. The obvious question is whether history will treat *Grutter* as an aberration that was limited to its unique facts, or whether it will be seen as the first step toward a new, post–*Brown v. Board of Education* approach to racial issues.

Shortly after *Grutter* was decided, the Supreme Court (having undergone some key departures and replacements) seemed to signal that *Grutter*'s approach to racial preferences would be narrowly construed, and that the decision itself might have a limited lifespan. In 2007, the Court invalidated two school district programs that considered race when assigning students to schools. One of the programs was designed

to maintain racial mixtures that roughly paralleled the larger community, and the other was intended to maintain prior desegregation efforts.
Both programs were found to be constitutionally infirm—not a good
sign for *Grutter* proponents.

Justice Kennedy Fakes Right and Goes Left: *Fisher v. University of Texas*

In 2008, Abigail Fisher, a white applicant who had been denied admission at the University of Texas sued the University, claiming that its
admission policy (which included the types of racial preferences that
had been approved in *Grutter*) was unconstitutional.

The case—*Fisher v. University of Texas*—came before the Supreme
Court in 2013. The fact that the Supreme Court decided to hear the
Fisher case only ten years after *Grutter* indicated a likely inclination to
revisit *Grutter* in some way, and the reason for that likely inclination was
very apparent: The pro-racial preference majority in *Grutter* had evaporated. Three of the justices who comprised the *Grutter* majority were no
longer on the Court, and Justice Kennedy, who remained on the Court,
had dissented in *Grutter*. In addition to Justice Kennedy, Chief Justice
Roberts and Justices Scalia, Thomas, and Alito had made their opposition
to racial preferences *very* plain in their prior rulings. Only Justices
Ginsburg, Breyer, Kagan, and Sotomayor favored *Grutter*-like racial preferences as a tool to promote diversity.

However, in a very unusual ruling issued after the 2013 arguments,
the Court refused to make a decision in *Fisher*. Justice Kennedy
explained the Court's rationale in an opinion to which six other justices
subscribed—only Justice Ginsburg dissented (Justice Kagan had
recused herself because she had been involved in the case when she
served as the United States Solicitor General).

In his opinion, Justice Kennedy was, as he had always been, skeptical about the constitutionality of racial preferences—he had never voted in favor of a racial preference or affirmative action—and he set the bar for approval of the University of Texas's racial-preference policy much higher than it had been set in *Grutter*. To uphold a racial-preference plan, Justice Kennedy wrote, the university would have to prove that "no workable race-neutral alternatives would produce the educational benefits of diversity." That is a *very* difficult burden to satisfy—how could the university prove that untried and hypothetical alternatives would *not* create the desired level of student diversity? To give the university an opportunity to meet this burden, the Court sent the case back to the Texas lower court for further proceedings.

On December 9, 2015, *Fisher* returned to the Court, and the lawyers presented their oral arguments. Justice Kennedy reviewed the evidence the university had introduced since his 2013 opinion, and he made it clear that he saw nothing new—the university had not met its burden in 2013, and despite having been given another opportunity to do so, it had not met its burden in 2015. He was plainly exasperated. "We're just arguing the same case," he told the lawyers.

Before the Court reached its final decision, Justice Scalia, an opponent of any racial preference, passed away. That left four justices (Roberts, Kennedy, Thomas, and Alito) whose prior opinions evidenced their general opposition to *Grutter*-like racial preferences, and three justices (Ginsburg, Breyer, and Sotomayor) who favored *Grutter*-like racial preferences. Among the *Grutter* opponents, Justice Kennedy left open the theoretical possibility that he might approve the university's racial-preference policy, but he had already shown his cards during the oral argument.

The writing was on the wall. The university's admission policy would be invalidated; *Grutter* would be reversed or extremely limited; and, implicitly or explicitly, racial preferences would be deemed unconstitutional.

Except it did not happen that way. Not even close. To the astonishment of virtually all of the pundits and his Supreme Court colleagues, Justice Kennedy reversed course. In his 2013 opinion, Justice Kennedy insisted that the university affirmatively *prove* that there were no other ways to achieve diversity. In his 2016 opinion, joined by Justices Ginsburg, Breyer, and Sotomayor, Justice Kennedy said that he was willing to accept the university's judgment, *whether or not* it was supported by the evidence. "Considerable deference," he wrote, "is owed to a university in defining those intangible characteristics, like student body diversity, that are central to its identity and educational mission."

Justice Alito, joined by Chief Justice Roberts and Justice Thomas, minced no words about Justice Kennedy's reversal—Justice Alito read his dissent from the bench, something a justice normally does only in the most important and controversial of cases. "Something strange has happened," Justice Alito wrote, "since our prior decision in this case." Without any factual basis to do so, he explained, "the majority concludes that U.T. has met its heavy burden. This conclusion is remarkable—and remarkably wrong."

Now What?

Laurence Tribe, a renowned constitutional law professor, summed up his view of *Fisher's* significance: "No decision since *Brown v. Board of Education*," he said, "has been as important as *Fisher* will prove to be in the long history of racial inclusion and educational diversity."

Maybe. But maybe not. If the events surrounding the effort to appoint a replacement for Justice Scalia teach us anything, it is this: In the current climate, whether Professor Tribe's prediction (or virtually any other prediction on the future of constitutional issues) turns out to be true will depend more on politics and less on an objective and dispassionate analysis of public policy and constitutional law.

For example, consider this scenario. If Justice Scalia's replacement supports racial preferences, then the pro–*Grutter/Fisher* justices will hold a 6–3 majority—two pro–*Grutter/Fisher* justices would have to be replaced by two anti-*Grutter/Fisher* justices for that majority to be lost. Theoretically, that could happen at any time, but the odds are that a two-justice switch of that kind could take decades to occur, if it ever occurs, and that could easily provide enough time for a pro–*Grutter/Fisher* majority to weave some form of racial preferences into the fabric of the country, making a reversal much more difficult and unlikely. In that event, *Fisher* may, indeed, become a foundational tenet of constitutional law.

Or, consider this scenario. If Justice Scalia's replacement opposes racial preferences, and if even one of the five pro–*Grutter/Fisher* justices are, in the next few years, replaced by a justice who is anti–*Grutter/Fisher* (Justices Ginsburg and Kennedy are both over eighty, and Justice Breyer is seventy-eight), then the impact of *Fisher* could be minimal and short-lived.

However this issue plays out in the coming years could very likely define how we deal with the monumentally important and difficult questions of affirmative action, racial preferences, and equal protection in contexts far beyond university admission policies. It could be argued that police departments, public school faculties, and government bureaucracies are more effective if they are diverse—that is, if they roughly parallel the racial, ethnic, and religious composition of the communities they serve. Will race, ethnicity, and religion then become part of local, state, and national government hiring protocols?

What about the private sector? Now businesses cannot discriminate in favor of or against any race, ethnicity, or religion in their hiring practices. But suppose businesses can prove that increasing diversity will enable them to better exploit global markets and keep pace with international competition—will they then be permitted to hire on the basis of race, ethnicity, and religion?

Grutter and *Fisher* have raised an array of immensely important societal questions surrounding minority preferences. For better or worse, it will be up to the Supreme Court—more precisely, the individuals who, through the vagaries of politics, are members of the Court when the issue next arises—to provide the answers to those questions.

CHAPTER 5

PLAYING POLITICS

"Politics is too serious a matter
to be left to the politicians."

—CHARLES DE GAULLE, PRESIDENT OF FRANCE, 1959–1969

Democracies gather legitimacy from the perception that their elections are fairly administered and free from undue influence. History documents that if the electoral process loses credibility, the fabric of a democracy quickly unravels.

Increasingly, however, Americans have come to believe that elections can be bought, not by (as in prior eras) stuffing the ballot box, but through the purchase of media time in such quantities as will steamroller an opponent of lesser means. But this concern—the concern for what has become known as "campaign finance reform"—runs headlong into a bedrock constitutional issue: can the government lawfully restrict the free speech rights of organizations to spend what they want to garner support for their preferred candidate?

There are other powers, as well, that the Supreme Court can use to assure the sanctity of our elections—as it attempted to do, with horrifically mixed reviews, in the 2000 presidential election.

Voters line up on Election Day in Clarendon, Virginia, 1924, to vote for president. Calvin Coolidge won the election.

11. The End of Meaningful Campaign Finance Reform?

Citizens United v. Federal Election Commission (2010)

Citizens United has joined the pantheon of cases in which the Supreme Court resolves a legal issue and, in the process, frames and ignites a deep, often corrosive, national debate. It is one of those cases whose name is a volatile proxy for the issues it addresses. *Brown v. Board of Education* denotes the advent of racial equality. *Roe v. Wade* represents the ongoing debate over abortion rights. *Citizens United* conjures the continuing, deep divide respecting campaign finance reform.

But, at the same time, it is much more than that. *Citizens United* has become a lightning rod for a cynical suspicion about the Supreme Court itself: Does the Court decide cases based on a dispassionate view of constitutional principles, or does it set out to serve a political bias or agenda?

The suspicion, whether justified or not, did not arise in a vacuum.

The Push for Campaign Finance Reform

During the 1990s, spurred by deepening public doubt about the integrity of the political process, Congress began to consider various legislative approaches in an effort to limit the influence of money in the political process. In 2002, after years of struggle and debate, Congress passed, and President Bush signed, the Bipartisan Campaign Reform Act (BCRA), popularly known as the "McCain-Feingold Act" in recognition of the bipartisan coalition that ultimately pushed the legislation over the finish line.

BCRA was considered a start, not the ultimate answer, to the problem of money and politics, particularly as the view that politicians who receive money might reward those who contribute money was repeatedly validated by well-publicized scandals. The special benefits Enron seemingly obtained from its massive campaign contributions gradually came to light. There was direct evidence of congressional corruption— the 2005 conviction of Congressman Randy "Duke" Cunningham for accepting $2.4 million in cash and yachts in exchange for defense contracts and, that same year, the discovery of $90,000 of marked bills, delivered by a federal informant and targeted for use in a bribery scheme, found hidden in Congressman William Jefferson's freezer.

Still, for example, Common Cause, a nonprofit advocacy group, reported that the health-care industry made $313.8 million in campaign contributions from 1989 to 2009, over half to members of Congress with jurisdiction over health-care reform, and in the first three months of 2009, thirty-four energy companies spent $23.7 million lobbying Congress on legislation that would affect standards for greenhouse gas emissions.

There was no consensus on how to limit the influence of big money, but at the time that *Citizens United* was decided, there was a vibrant and ongoing debate that took as an article of faith the fact that, somehow, it had to be done.

How the *Citizens United* Case Arose

Citizens United is a "super PAC"—a nonprofit corporation that solicits money to support or oppose candidates for office. ("PAC" is an acronym for "political action committee." Super PACs are unique, in that, unlike other PACs, they can solicit unlimited amounts of money from a variety of individual and corporate sources, but they can only spend the money independently and cannot contribute directly to a candidate or party.) It produced a scathing movie about Hillary Clinton and aired it during her 2008 presidential campaign.

Citizens United wanted to make the movie available by video-on-demand within thirty days of the 2008 primary elections, but it knew that a section of BCRA prohibited corporations, including nonprofit corporations such as Citizens United (but not individuals), from using their money to distribute "electioneering communications"—that is, communications that advocate for or against a candidate—within sixty days of a general election and thirty days of a primary election.

Congress's point in creating this restriction was plain. By their nature, corporations, especially large corporations, can accumulate vast amounts of money, and Congress found that the electoral "level playing field" on which any democracy depends could be unfairly tilted toward corporate interests if corporations were permitted to use this wealth to support selected candidates.

Citizens United challenged the legality of the application of BCRA to its movie. A lower court upheld BCRA and ruled against Citizens United, and by 2009 the case made its way to the Supreme Court.

The Law, Pre–*Citizens United*

Citizens United had a steep hill to climb. For over one hundred years, Congress had prohibited the kinds of politics-driven corporate expenditures Citizens United was making. In 1907, Congress passed the Tillman Act, which banned corporate electioneering expenses. (The Tillman Act was born out of the 1896 presidential race, in which William McKinley ran against William Jennings Bryan. McKinley's campaign was funded by many of the nation's largest corporations, and he outspent Bryan 10–1, prompting Bryan's campaign manager to famously observe, "There are two things that are important in politics. The first is money, and I can't remember what the second one is.") Congress ultimately expanded the reach of the Tillman Act by enacting the Federal Corrupt Practices Act, which led to BCRA in 2002. These restrictions on corporate political spending had survived all manner of court scrutiny for decades.

In addition, in 2003, only a few years before *Citizens United*, the Supreme Court upheld this aspect of BCRA in *McConnell v. Federal Election Commission*—Citizens United faced a recent, clear Supreme Court precedent that specifically ruled against the position it was espousing.

But despite all of this, and even though the ink on the *McConnell* decision had hardly dried, Citizens United thought it had a strong case. *McConnell* was decided by a 5–4 vote. Two of the "yes" votes, Justice O'Connor and Justice Souter, had since retired. By the time Citizens United brought its case, Justice O'Connor and Justice Souter had been replaced by two very likely "no" votes: Chief Justice Roberts and Justice Alito. Justice Kennedy, Justice Scalia, and Justice Thomas had already shown their cards—they had dissented in *McConnell*.

Citizens United might not have had Supreme Court precedent on its side. But it knew how to count Supreme Court votes.

The Law, Post–*Citizens United*

Citizens United was decided by yet another Roberts Court 5–4 majority. Justice Kennedy, assuming his frequent role as the swing vote, wrote the majority opinion, and he (and the usual "conservative" bloc of Justices Roberts, Scalia, Alito, and Thomas who joined with him) chose to cast the *Citizens United* issues in First Amendment terms, as a question of free speech. (This provoked many critics of the majority to accuse it of unwarranted judicial activism—they claim that true "conservative" justices would have decided the case on much narrower grounds, based on an interpretation of BCRA, not the First Amendment.)

Having chosen to focus on whether Citizens United had a First Amendment right to air the movie, the majority still had to clear a substantial hurdle. The First Amendment prohibits the government from "abridging the freedom of speech." But unlike the usual situation, here it was Citizens United, a corporation and not a person, asserting a constitutional right of free speech. Do corporations (as opposed to, for example, the people who own them or run them) engage in "speech"? And if a corporation can speak, is the corporation covered by the First Amendment as if it were a person?

Justice Kennedy attacked this issue by concluding that it was not really an issue at all. He stressed the vital importance of protecting the right of free speech without regard for the source of the speech — individual, corporation, powerful, oppressed, or otherwise. He quoted precedent: "The identity of the speaker is not decisive in determining whether speech is protected. Corporations and other associations, like individuals, contribute to the 'discussion, debate, and the dissemination of information and ideas' that the First Amendment seeks to foster." Were this provision of BCRA enforced against any speaker who chose to express a preference for a political candidate, he wrote, "Speech would be suppressed in the realm where its necessity is most evident: in the public dialogue preceding a real election."

Justice Kennedy also disagreed with the primary rationale for limiting corporate expenditures — that money buys access and promotes corruption. He opined that only evidence of quid pro quo corruption — a direct payment for a specific act in return — would justify curbing corporate expenditures, and for that reason, large, direct contributions to candidates could be prohibited as being justifiably suspicious. But, he concluded, there was no evidence that indirect support of a candidate — like distributing a movie excoriating a candidate's opponent — would lead to corruption. "There is only scant evidence that independent expenditures" might ingratiate a corporation to a candidate, he said, but "ingratiation and access, in any event, are not corruption."

Citizens United dealt only with indirect corporate expenditures (that is, not direct contributions to a candidate), like the money Citizens United spent to produce and distribute its movie. There are (or were— more about that soon) federal and state laws that, in some circumstances, prohibit corporations from contributing directly to a candidate, and those laws were not affected. In addition, the *Citizens United* majority left intact certain campaign expenditure disclosure requirements in BCRA.

The Dissent

Justice Stevens wrote an eighty-seven-page dissent in which the three other justices joined. His dissent has become the brief for the opponents of *Citizens United*.

Justice Stevens confronted the majority's conflation of corporations and people. "Although they make enormous contributions to our society, corporations are not actually members of it. They cannot vote or run for office. Because they may be managed and controlled by non-residents, their interests may conflict in fundamental respects with the interests of eligible voters. The financial resources, legal structure, and instrumental orientation of corporations raise legitimate concerns about their role in the electoral process." He quoted from several prior cases in which the Supreme Court had plainly stated that "legislatures are entitled to decide 'that the special characteristics of the corporate structure require particularly careful regulation' in an electoral context."

Justice Stevens argued that, in any event, First Amendment protection has never been absolute, and he cited a litany of cases which carved out exceptions to the First Amendment when justified by a legitimate government interest—such as, he suggested, the government's interest in quelling the influence of corporate money in the political system.

He scoffed at the majority's conclusion—which, he pointed out, was not backed by any evidence or data—that buying access does not lead to corruption. "In an age in which money and television ads are the coin of the campaign realm, it is hardly surprising that corporations deployed these ads to curry favor with, and to gain influence over, public officials."

The Reaction: The Rights of Corporations and the Risks to Fair Elections

In the aftermath of the *Citizens United* decision, there has been no shortage of impeccably qualified, nonpartisan and well-respected First Amendment lawyers and scholars who have celebrated it as a courageous defense of First Amendment rights. And there has been a cascade of equally qualified and respected lawyers and legal scholars who deride the decision as a convoluted stretch, a strained effort to fit the round peg of corporate electioneering activities into the square hole of the First Amendment.

But apart from the lawyers and legal scholars, *Citizens United* has spawned a storm of rancorous criticism—most people (according to survey data) believe that the decision fosters a system in which elected officials, even if not quid pro quo corrupt, are highly influenced by corporations that provide the money it takes to get elected and stay elected in a political system dominated by expensive television commercials and political consultants.

In February 2010, just one month after *Citizens United* was decided, a *Washington Post*–ABC News poll found that 85 percent of Democrats, 76 percent of Republicans, and 81 percent of independents opposed the decision, including large majorities of those with household incomes both above and below $50,000. Age, race, and education levels had little relationship to the poll results.

In January 2012, the Pew Research Center reported that "Fully 65 percent of those who are aware of the new rules on independent expenditures say they are having a negative effect on the 2012 presidential campaign. And among those who have heard a lot about these new campaign finance rules, 78 percent say the effect has been negative." There was no substantial difference between Republicans and Democrats.

By 2015, 78 percent of those responding to a Bloomberg Politics national poll said *Citizens United* should be overruled.

Much has been written about the fact that the Court simply dismissed, as if not worth serious consideration, the idea that corruption can take other forms, as when a corporation in a regulated industry funds ads supporting a congressman who sits on the committee that administers those regulations. Justice Stevens presaged what the polls seem to confirm. He stated in his dissent, "At bottom, the Court's opinion is thus a rejection of the common sense of the American people, who have recognized a need to prevent corporations from undermining self-government since the founding, and who have fought against the distinctive corrupting potential of corporate electioneering since the days of Theodore Roosevelt."

Should that matter? Supreme Court decisions are not supposed to be based on polling data or amorphous conceptions of common sense. The Supreme Court is to hold fast to the law, no matter what the majority might prefer, no matter the level of public outcry. Still, many critics of the decision continue to ask an important question: Did the *Citizens United* majority decide the case on the basis of the law, or did they preordain a result based on their policy preferences?

The way in which the Court reached its decision has played a role in fueling these accusations. As has so often occurred among the Roberts Court's 5–4 decisions, the so-called "conservative" and "liberal" justices voted as a predictable bloc. But, contrary to form, the conservatives effectively switched roles with the liberals: they decided the case on much broader constitutional grounds than were required, they invalidated over one hundred years of statutory law, and they overruled a virtually brand-new Supreme Court decision. The supposedly nonactivist conservatives did what they usually accuse the supposedly activist liberals of doing.

Why would the majority seemingly violate their judicial principles? To many, the answer is because, at the time, it was the only way to get where they wanted to go.

For example, Thomas E. Mann, a senior fellow at the Brookings Institution, wrote that "the Roberts Court is dead set on deregulating campaign finance."

"The court got way, way, way ahead of its skis here," said Rhode Island Democratic Senator Sheldon Whitehouse in 2012. "It was a decision they were so eager to make, but now I think they're embarrassed by the wild discrepancy between the world as they presumed it in their written decision and the world as we see it around us, post–*Citizens United.*"

Controversial Supreme Court decisions are routinely challenged, even excoriated. There is nothing wrong with that. But in respect to *Citizens United* (like *Brown v. Board of Education* and *Roe v. Wade*, for example), there has been a disconcerting level of commentary arguing that there is a basis on which to question not only the Court's wisdom, but its motives.

The Progeny of *Citizens United:* Are There Any Meaningful Restrictions Left?

Citizens United's "hands-off" approach to indirect corporate campaign expenditures gave birth to further cases, which ultimately led to the rising role of super PACs in American elections.

SpeechNow is a super PAC that solicits contributions from individuals to support its development and placement of ads that support or oppose candidates. It challenged the constitutionality of the Federal Election Campaign Act, which limited the amount that individuals could contribute to any PAC to $5,000 annually. Shortly after *Citizens United* was decided and in reliance on it, the United States Court of Appeals for the District of Columbia Circuit—a highly influential appeals court that ranks just below the Supreme Court—ruled that the contribution limits were unconstitutional, and that there were to be no limits on the amounts that individuals could contribute to super PACs.

The result: Corporations and individuals have the unlimited right to contribute as much money as they want to organizations that support and oppose political candidates.

The aftermath has been predictable, though the debate continues over the effects of the aftermath on electoral politics. For instance, in June 2012, wealthy businessman Sheldon Adelson and his wife gave $10 million to a super PAC that supported Mitt Romney. According to a December 20, 2012, article in *ProPublica*, a nonprofit focusing on investigative journalism, during the 2012 election cycle, the Adelsons' reported contributions amounted to approximately $98 million. According to OpenSecrets.org (a Center for Responsive Politics website that tracks federal campaign contributions), in the 2014 midterm campaign, 1,360 super PACs raised nearly $700 million.

Super PACs are required to disclose the names of their contributors (although substantial delays are built into the system). But there are other, more secretive avenues for the influx of big money into politics—"social welfare" groups formed pursuant to section 501(c)4 of the Internal Revenue Code being the current, classic example.

501(c)4 organizations abound, for all the right reasons—a local fire company or land conservation group would be prototypical 501(c)4 organizations. However, so long as a 501(c)4 organization spends less than 50 percent of its money on politics, it can solicit political contributions and make campaign contributions to super PACs, and it is not required to disclose the names of its donors. Smart political operatives saw the potential—for example, Crossroads GPS, founded by Karl Rove, and Organizing for Action, which advocated for President Obama.

Thus was born the "dark money" campaign contribution. As reported in the same *ProPublica* article, two Republican fundraisers told the press that the Adelsons contributed an additional $45 million during the 2012 election cycle to "dark money" groups that were not required to disclose their donors.

Closing the loop, if not the loopholes, in 2014, the Supreme Court decided the case of *McCutcheon v. FEC*. In still another party-line 5–4 vote (the usual four conservative votes joined by Justice Kennedy), the Court, in an opinion by Chief Justice Roberts, invalidated BCRA's limit on the $123,000 total amount an individual may contribute to all candidates and PACs in any one election cycle, but the $5,200 limit on the amount of each contribution to each candidate and PAC was retained—so donors can make as many $5,200 contributions as they want to as many candidates and PACs as they want. The cracks in that judicial edifice were obvious—what if your local congressional candidate is supported by twenty different super PACs?

Here is, perhaps, the most interesting aspect to *Citizens United* and its aftermath: It could all disappear almost overnight. All it would take would be the replacement of one Republican appointee with one Democratic appointee who takes a definitive stand in favor of campaign finance reform principles. That would probably create a 5–4 majority that believes in the constitutionality of campaign finance reform and does not believe that corporations have the same First Amendment rights as individuals.

Just as the *Citizens United* majority had no compunctions about reversing the recently decided *McConnell* precedent that stood in its way, this new majority, should it eventuate, may relegate *Citizens United* to a historical footnote.

12. Did the Supreme Court Play Politics in the 2000 Election?

Bush v. Gore (2000)

In the view of many, the Supreme Court elected George W. Bush the president of the United States.

After the ballots were counted in the November 7, 2000, presidential election, Al Gore led Bush in the popular vote, and Gore led the electoral-college vote by a 267–246 margin. Whoever reached 270 electoral votes would win the presidency. The only state still in play was Florida, whose 25 electoral votes would go to the candidate who won the Florida popular vote. The initial Florida vote count had Bush leading Gore, 2,909,135 votes to 2,907,351, but because the margin was less than 0.5 percent, Florida law required a machine recount. The machine recount reduced Bush's margin to a scant 327 votes.

Gore, as was his right according to Florida law, then requested a manual recount in four Florida counties. The law, however, mandated that the recount be completed in seven days. This led three of the counties to request more time to complete the manual recount, but Florida's secretary of state, Katherine Harris, believing that an extension would be unlawful, refused the request. Gore disagreed with Harris's position, filed a lawsuit, and the legal dispute that eventually became *Bush v. Gore* was born.

In short order, Gore's case was argued before the Florida Supreme Court, which issued an order requiring Harris to allow the requested extension, through November 26. Bush appealed that ruling to the U.S. Supreme Court, which requested certain clarifications before it would rule. In the interim, one of the counties, Miami-Dade, canceled its manual recount, stating that it could not complete the recount by the November 26 deadline.

On November 26, despite the incomplete recount, Harris certified Bush as the winner by only 537 votes—thereby awarding Bush Florida's 25 electoral votes and the presidency.

On November 27, Gore filed another suit to contest the certified results of the election. He lost, and again appealed to the Florida Supreme Court which, on December 8, ordered a state-wide manual recount. Bush again appealed to the U.S. Supreme Court, which issued an injunction stopping the statewide recount, pending its final decision.

On December 11, the Supreme Court heard oral arguments. Just sixteen hours later, with the presidency in the balance and the nation on the edge of its seat, the Court rendered its opinion.

Hanging Chads, Dimpled Chads, and Equal Protection

The Supreme Court tied most of its analysis to the Equal Protection Clause of the Fourteenth Amendment to the Constitution, which provides that "No State shall . . . deny to any person . . . the equal protection of the laws." In the wake of televised accounts of election commissioners squinting through magnifying glasses, some finding significance in "hanging chads," others being influenced by "dimpled chads," Bush argued that there was no uniform vote-counting standard among the various Florida counties and, therefore, two voters in different counties could mark their ballots in an identical manner, and one would be counted while the other would be disregarded. This, said Bush, was a denial of equal protection, and the recount should be halted on that basis.

Gore argued that equal protection does not require absolute uniformity, and because all of the Florida counties subscribed to one standard—trying to derive the intent of the voters who marked the ballots—the Equal Protection Clause was satisfied. Gore pointed out that every state uses a variety of different methods to record votes in different counties, ranging from optical scanners to punch cards. Therefore, said Gore, if Bush prevailed, from that day forward every state would have to implement a uniform system of voting in order to satisfy constitutional standards, which was neither required under the law, nor possible as a matter of stark reality.

The Supreme Court's decision was a hodgepodge of arcane legal reasoning and varying alliances among varying justices on varying points, but the upshot was that Bush won. Essentially, the majority of justices ruled that the different vote-counting techniques undertaken in the recount were constitutionally problematic. This meant that the manual recount had to cease, and the election results had to be certified as they existed prior to the recount. Bush assumed the presidency on the strength of that opinion.

The Criticism from Without, and from Within

Bush v. Gore touched off an immediate explosion of political commentary, although, not surprisingly, in most instances those politicians who favored the Court's reasoning were prior adherents of Bush or his philosophies, and vice versa.

In addition, constitutional law scholars quickly emerged from their ivory towers. While some supported the decision, those who garnered the most media attention vituperatively denounced the legal underpinnings of the *Bush v. Gore* decision, often charging that the justices voted their politics, not the law. American University law professor Jamin Raskin wrote in the *Washington Monthly* that *Bush v. Gore* was "quite demonstrably the worst Supreme Court decision in history," even worse than the infamous *Dred Scott* decision. Harvard law professor Laurence Tribe, one of the country's most respected constitutional scholars (and one of the attorneys who represented Gore), wrote that the Court's opinion "cannot be grounded in any previously recognizable form of equal protection doctrine." Another Harvard law professor, Randall Kennedy, labeled the decision a "hypocritical mishmash of ideas." Mincing no words on his view of why the majority ruled as it did, Sanford Levinson, a University of Texas law professor, wrote in *The Nation* that the decision was "easily explainable" as the decision of Republican justices who intended "to assure the triumph of a fellow Republican who might not become president if Florida were left to its own legal process."

Perhaps most disturbing, however, was the fact that allegations of this type, charging nothing short of judicial corruption, were not limited to pundits and professors. In divisive matters of national importance that consume the nation's attention, the Supreme Court strives for a unanimous opinion in the effort to speak with one voice and promote national unity. When, as in *Bush v. Gore*, that cannot be achieved, Supreme Court justices will normally characterize their disagreements as good-faith disputes over legal precedents or philosophy. Very rarely will they question each other's motives or integrity. In *Bush v. Gore*, however, Justice Stevens, one of the dissenters, used startling language to characterize his view of what the Court's majority had done. He wrote that the majority's position "can only lend credence to the most cynical appraisal of the work of judges throughout the land. It is confidence in the men and women who administer the judicial system that is the true backbone of the rule of law. Time will one day heal the wound to that confidence that will be inflicted by today's decision. One thing, however, is certain. Although we may never know with complete certainty the identity of the winner of this year's Presidential election, the identity of the loser is perfectly clear. It is the Nation's confidence in the judge as an impartial guardian of the rule of law."

In advance of the 2004 presidential election, many had predicted that whoever lost would challenge the results based on the *Bush v. Gore* ruling that disparate vote-counting procedures could violate the Equal Protection Clause, and that the nation would then be thrown into tumult. Obviously, that did not happen. Still, voter confidence in the electoral system—a linchpin of any democracy—has shown problematic and continuing weaknesses. According to a 2008 study by the Pew Research Center, only 57 percent of Americans were "very confident" that their votes will be counted accurately—down from 62 percent in 2004. About 10 percent of the voters expressed little confidence in our voting system.

The 2008 presidential election was not close enough to cause doubts about the outcome based on voting inaccuracies, but it is certainly foreseeable that another too-close-to-call vote could emerge in a future election, resulting in a *Bush v. Gore*–like lawsuit. In 2006, for example, a Court of Appeals declared unconstitutional the use of different voting technologies in different Ohio counties because under one system voters were given the opportunity to find and correct mistakes they made on their ballot before casting their vote, and in another system they were not given that opportunity. Until the Supreme Court says otherwise, the analytical framework endorsed by the majority in *Bush v. Gore* continues to bind lower courts, creating the potential for similar election challenges in the future.

Especially in view of the changing makeup of the Court since 2000, it is impossible to predict whether the Supreme Court itself will again delve into the electoral process, or instead leave it to the states to untangle their own messes (as the dissenting justices argued the Court should have done in 2000). In a much different context, involving federal law and not states' rights, the Court was anything but reluctant to involve itself in a monumental voting controversy. In its 2013 decision in *Shelby v. Holder*, the Court's "conservative" bloc of justices overruled

Congress's decision to maintain in effect the heart of the Voting Rights Act which, based on prior discrimination, had prohibited nine states from changing their election laws without federal government approval. Justice Ginsburg wrote in her dissent that the Court should have deferred to Congress, which in 2006 had reauthorized the law by a large majority (390 to 33 in the House, unanimously in the Senate). A 5–4 majority—since labeled "activist" by its critics—disagreed.

Justice Scalia, for his part, has since expressed the view that *Bush v. Gore* is old news. When asked about the continuing penchant of many to decry the decision, his response was, "It's water over the deck—get over it." Easier said than done—if faced with a similar case in the future, the then-sitting justices will, no doubt, be mindful of the firestorm *Bush v. Gore* ignited, and it would not be surprising if, at that time, the Court looked for a way out, instead of a way in.

Whether *Bush v. Gore* will cause the American people to doubt the ostensibly apolitical nature of the Supreme Court in the future will likely depend on how the justices on the Court, especially the post-2000 appointees, acquit themselves in the public eye. If future decisions are perceived as exercises in which they strain to reach results that conform with their known predispositions, that will lead to one type of public perception, and comparisons to *Bush v. Gore* will be inevitable. If those decisions reflect objectivity and legal scholarship that lead to results that support no particular political or policy point of view, *Bush v. Gore* will likely be viewed as an historical anomaly, a one-time-only aberration with extreme political but limited precedential significance.

CHAPTER 6

THE RIGHT TO DO WHAT YOU WANT

*"The right to be let alone is indeed
the beginning of all freedom."*

—WILLIAM O. DOUGLAS, SUPREME COURT JUSTICE, 1939–75

Justice Douglas was a staunch supporter of individual rights, but, as even he would concede, the yearning to be let alone must have its limits. As Justice Oliver Wendell Holmes Jr. put it, "The right to swing my fist ends where the other man's nose begins."

Still, Justice Holmes's commonsense rule creates its own conundrum: it is not always so easy to determine just where the other man's figurative nose really is.

Sometimes, of course, the line is obvious—you can't steal money or pollute a river. But what about an individual who chooses to live his private life in a way that harms no one else, but violates the majority's principles or sensibilities? On what basis would one group's moral or religious beliefs in opposition to, for instance, suicide or same-sex marriage, take precedence over another group's moral or religious beliefs to the contrary? What defines "the land of the free" if not the the freedom to make one's own life choices?

Estelle Griswold, executive director of Planned Parenthood, is pictured in front of the Connecticut center in April 1963; the center was closed pending decision of the U.S. Supreme Court in *Griswold v. Connecticut.*

13. The Unwritten Right of Privacy

Griswold v. Connecticut (1965)

In *Griswold v. Connecticut*, the Supreme Court found within the Constitution a new and fundamental right: the right of privacy. In the process, the Supreme Court created the legal foundation on which, eight years later, *Roe v. Wade* was built, and on which other, as yet unforeseen, judicial results may also be founded. In addition, the *Griswold* case set off a conflagration, which continues through today, over the proper role of a Supreme Court justice in American society.

The background for the *Griswold* case goes back to 1879, when Connecticut passed a law outlawing contraception and making it a crime to use, or to assist or counsel anyone to use, "any drug, medicinal article or instrument for the purpose of preventing conception." The law was almost never enforced, but many persons found it an offensive intrusion into their personal lives and wanted it off the books.

In the effort to create a test case to challenge the constitutionality of the law, Estelle Griswold, executive director of the Planned Parenthood League of Connecticut, and Dr. C. Lee Buxton, a physician and professor at the Yale School of Medicine, opened a birth-control clinic in New Haven. Shortly thereafter, they were arrested, tried, found guilty, and fined $100. They appealed, and the Supreme Court eventually agreed to hear their case.

Constitution or Conscience?

Sometimes a judge is presented with a case where justice and common sense cry out for a particular result, but there's no obvious law that allows the judge to get where he desperately wants to go. *Griswold* was that type of case. The vast majority of citizens, and all of the Supreme Court justices involved in *Griswold*, felt that the Connecticut law was an absurd and even repugnant invasion of the lives of married couples. Yet there was no apparent constitutional hook on which to hang the argument that the Connecticut statute was invalid.

Some justices, when faced with that kind of a case, view their sworn role as being limited to the enforcement of the Constitution as written, no matter the unfairness that may result in a particular situation. Their rationale is that if we are to remain a "government of laws and not men," some injustices may have to be suffered in order to avoid a greater evil—the creation of a judiciary in which justices are free to make up the law as they go along in order to dispense their own brands of situational equity.

Other justices, however, view their role much differently. They view the law in general, and the Constitution in particular, as a living, evolving rule book that has to change as society changes and as new, unforeseen situations are presented. They acknowledge an obligation to stay as close as feasible to the intent of the Constitution as written, but they view it as their duty to stretch its language in order to do what justice requires.

Penumbras and Emanations

Justice Douglas wrote the majority opinion in *Griswold*. He was an individualist who enthusiastically subscribed to the view that the law should be expanded when required to protect individual rights.

Justice Douglas conceded that the word "privacy" appears nowhere in the Constitution. Nevertheless, he concluded that, at least insofar as married couples are concerned, a fundamental right of privacy is implicit in the various guaranties given in the Bill of Rights, the first ten amendments to the Constitution. In some of the most famous (and ridiculed) language ever written by a Supreme Court justice, he offered that "specific guarantees in the Bill of Rights have penumbras, formed by emanations from those guarantees that help give them life and substance." For instance, the Fourth Amendment precludes unreasonable searches and seizures, which implies a right of privacy. The Fifth Amendment gives citizens the right against self-incrimination, which Justice Douglas likened to a personal "zone of privacy."

Two justices, Hugo Black and Potter Stewart, held judicial philosophies vastly different than Douglas's, and dissented. Justice Black found the Connecticut law "offensive." Justice Stewart called it "uncommonly silly." But that alone, they wrote, did not make it unconstitutional. Justice Black went on, "The Court talks about a constitutional 'right of privacy' as though there is some constitutional provision or provisions forbidding any law ever to be passed which might abridge the 'privacy' of individuals. But there is not." He concluded, "I like my privacy as well as the next one, but I am nevertheless compelled to admit that government has a right to invade it unless prohibited by some specific constitutional provision."

Griswold's Unintended Consequences

Griswold is extremely important for at least two reasons: what the justices said in the case; and what the justices did in the case.

Concerning what was said in *Griswold*, by creating a new and fundamental right of privacy, *Griswold* provided a means for future Supreme Court justices to reach ends that were previously unreachable. The prime example is, of course, *Roe v. Wade*. In addition, however, *Griswold* was used as the legal justification for the Court to strike down laws barring the sale of contraceptives to unmarried couples in 1972; in 2003, in the case of *Lawrence v. Texas*, the Supreme Court, building on *Griswold* without really admitting it, declared unconstitutional a state sodomy law and in the process invalidated all laws seeking to regulate intimate contact among adults.

Concerning what was done in *Griswold*, those who believe that the Constitution must be broadly interpreted to adjust to changing times were heartened, and those who believe that the Constitution must be strictly construed according to its language or, at most, the known intent of the framers, were outraged. Thanks in large part to *Griswold*, the judicial school of thought favored by a prospective justice has become a near-litmus test for those nominated to the Supreme Court. In their Senate confirmation hearings, prospective justices are routinely asked if they believe in a constitutional right to privacy. This is code for a question that asks, in one sense, if they would interpret the Constitution broadly or strictly and, in another sense, if they might consider reversing *Roe v. Wade*.

14. Does the Right of Privacy Include the Right to an Abortion?

Roe v. Wade (1973)
Planned Parenthood v. Casey (1992)
Whole Woman's Health v. Hellerstedt (2016)

Roe v. Wade is one of the most vigorously debated and politically sensitive Supreme Court decisions in American history. It arose out of a Texas statute that, like statutes in many other states, prohibited abortions except for the medical purpose of saving the mother's life. Roe, an unmarried pregnant woman who sought an abortion, filed a lawsuit in which she claimed the statute was unconstitutional, and the case was ultimately heard by the Supreme Court.

Roe won her case. Justice Harry Blackmun, joined by six other justices, ruled that the Constitution permits a woman to decide for herself whether to terminate her pregnancy, although the state could regulate abortion procedures in order to safeguard the woman's health and maintain medical standards. It is only when the fetus becomes able to live outside the womb, the Court ruled, that states may prohibit abortions, except those abortions required to preserve the life or health of the mother.

The fact that the justices were passionately at odds over *Roe*, and remain so, is well known. Justice Byron White, among others, wrote a withering dissent. "I find nothing in the language or history of the Constitution to support the Court's judgment . . . its judgment is an improvident and extravagant exercise of the power of judicial review that the Constitution extends to this Court." Justice Rehnquist wrote that the *Roe* majority based their decision on a supposed right that was "completely unknown" to the drafters of the Constitution.

In particular, two aspects of *Roe v. Wade* continue to stir wide-ranging fervor and controversy.

First, the Court refused to rule that, under the Constitution, an unborn child is a "person" entitled to constitutional protections. *Roe* is largely responsible for the raging political debate over when life begins, even though it failed to make a meaningful attempt to engage in the debate it created.

Second, the Court based much of its logic on a "right to privacy" that prior cases (like the *Griswold v. Connecticut* decision discussed earlier) found to exist within the Constitution, even though no such right is set forth in the Constitution in so many words. Using *Griswold* and similar cases as a legal stepping-stone, *Roe* expanded the newfound right to privacy "to encompass a woman's decision whether or not to terminate her pregnancy." Many commentators find the notion that the Constitution includes a fundamental right of privacy to be more fabrication than interpretation, and they further find the extension of that supposed right to abortion to be a logical and moral non sequitur. Others, of course, vehemently disagree.

Roe's Future, and the Future of Abortion

Despite the ongoing controversy, *Roe*'s central holding—that a woman has a right to an abortion up until the time the fetus is viable—has stood the test of time, albeit with certain exceptions. In a pivotal 1992 decision, *Planned Parenthood v. Casey*, the Court reaffirmed its commitment to *Roe*, but conceded that certain restrictions on the right of abortion could be constitutional—*so long as* the restrictions did not place "an undue burden" on the right of a woman to obtain an abortion before the fetus attains viability. That "undue burden" standard has remained the touchstone on which the constitutionality of legislative and judicial efforts to restrict abortion rights has been determined.

But, of course, "undue" is in the eye of the beholder. In this instance, the beholder is the Supreme Court—more precisely, the members of the Court at the time an abortion challenge is raised.

In June 2016, the Supreme Court issued its long-awaited opinion in *Whole Woman's Health v. Hellerstedt*, the most significant abortion case since *Planned Parenthood*. *Whole Woman's Health* involved a challenge to a Texas law which, its proponents claimed, was enacted to protect the health of women who choose to undergo an abortion. The law placed two new requirements on Texas abortion facilities: first, any physician who performed an abortion had to have admitting privileges at a hospital located within thirty miles of the abortion facility; second, abortion facilities were required to meet the minimum standards for ambulatory surgical centers. The *Whole Woman's Health* decision provides a window into how at least five of the current justices view the "undue burden" standard now, and how abortion issues may be dealt with in the future.

Justice Breyer, joined by Justices Kennedy, Ginsburg, Sotomayor, and Kagan, wrote the majority opinion. Justice Breyer found that the Texas law served no health-related purpose; the evidence documented that abortion was already an extremely safe procedure with very low rates of complications and virtually no deaths. The *real* purpose and effect of the law, he concluded, was not to promote women's health, but to make it exponentially more difficult for women to obtain an abortion by drastically reducing the number of abortion facilities that could afford to operate in Texas. After the law was enacted in 2013, the number of Texas abortion facilities dropped from forty to twenty. The cost to comply with the surgical-center requirement would most likely exceed $1.5 million to $3 million per clinic, and would reduce the number of clinics to seven or eight. The number of woman of reproductive age living more than 200 miles away from an abortion facility had increased by about 2,800 percent.

Justice Breyer's conclusion: The Texas law "poses a substantial obstacle to women seeking abortions, and constitutes an 'undue burden' on their constitutional right to do so."

Chief Justice Roberts, Justice Alito, and Justice Thomas dissented (the case was decided before the appointment of a replacement for Justice Scalia, accounting for the 5–3 vote). Justice Alito wrote that, whether or not one favors or disfavors the right of abortion, the Supreme Court had no procedural right to invalidate the Texas law, and the Court had seriously overreached its authority by doing so. "When we decide cases on particularly controversial issues, we should take special care to apply settled procedural rules in a neutral manner," Justice Alito wrote. "The Court has not done that here."

Justice Thomas went a step further (and, interestingly, neither Chief Justice Roberts nor Justice Alito joined in his opinion). Justice Thomas charged that, contrary to basic constitutional principles, the majority had vested the right to abortion with an inexplicably favored status among constitutional rights, and had gone out of its way, in violation of law, to achieve its "undue burden" conclusion. Quoting from a prior opinion by Justice Scalia, Justice Thomas wrote that the *Whole Woman's Health* "decision exemplifies the Court's troubling tendency 'to bend the rules when any effort to limit abortion, or even to speak in opposition to abortion, is at issue.'"

The *Whole Woman's Health* case tells us that, in 2016, five justices hold *Roe v. Wade* as established law, and will vigorously (perhaps too much so, according to the dissenters) scrutinize efforts to restrict the right of abortion. Where, precisely, each justice stands in respect to what does and does not cross the "undue burden" line remains less clear. As for the future, the potential for redefining the "undue burden" test, limiting *Roe*, or even reversing *Roe* will most likely depend on which justices leave the Court, and which party controls the presidency and the Senate when they do so.

15. The Right to Die

Washington v. Glucksberg (1997)

Suppose a close friend becomes terminally ill, all quality of life has evaporated, and he is suffering. Moreover, his medical bills will dissipate his assets, and he is desperately worried about his family's financial future. He tells you he would prefer to die—peacefully, without pain, now. He pleads with you, as his closest friend, to help him carry out his wishes. All you need to do is fill an old painkiller prescription he has, give him the bottle, and he will do the rest. May you do it? May you arrange for a doctor or nurse to help him, and even if you could, would they be permitted to do anything?

As of this writing, forty-nine states prohibit assisted suicide, and in recent years doctors, terminally ill patients, and "death with dignity" organizations have challenged the constitutionality of these laws in court. One such challenge was mounted in the mid-1990s by Dr. Harold Glucksberg, along with other physicians, patients, and a nonprofit advocacy group. It involved a Washington state statute that makes "promoting a suicide" a felony. Glucksberg sought the right to honor the wishes of terminal patients who asked for his assistance. The case, *Washington v. Glucksberg*, made its way to the Supreme Court in 1997.

The Limits of Liberty

Glucksberg, like most litigants who have challenged assisted-suicide bans, based his case on the historic Due Process Clause of the Fourteenth Amendment, which prohibits a state from depriving persons of "life, liberty, or property without due process of law." Surely,

Glucksberg contended, this constitutional right of liberty must include the right of a competent adult to choose to die, and to seek assistance in implementing that decision. As the saying goes, it's a free country.

Some lower courts had agreed with this argument in other cases, but the Supreme Court, in an opinion written by Chief Justice Rehnquist, unanimously disagreed. The Court found that the Due Process Clause does not prevent government from regulating all conceivable liberties, but only certain fundamental liberties rooted in the nation's history and traditions. The Court reviewed Anglo-American law since the 1400s, and found that England, and then the colonies, had prohibited assisted suicides for hundreds of years. Therefore, the Court ruled, there was no reason to believe that the framers of the Constitution intended to contravene this tradition and establish a "right to die." Consequently, said the Court, it was not unconstitutional for a state to criminalize assisted suicide.

Keep in mind, however, that while *Washington v. Glucksberg* stands for the proposition that states may lawfully prohibit assisted suicides within their borders, states may, conversely, allow assisted suicides if they wish. In 1997, Oregon enacted the Death with Dignity Act, which permits physicians, in well-defined circumstances, to provide a lethal dosage of pills to terminally ill patients who seek to end their own suffering. It is then up to the patient to take the pills, or not. The Bush administration challenged the constitutionality of the Death with Dignity Act and, in January 2006, the Supreme Court, while not endorsing the law, refused to overturn it, in a 6–3 vote. Several other states then enacted their own "death with dignity" laws, including Washington, Vermont, and Montana, and similar laws are pending in several other states. A May 2013 Gallup survey found "70 percent of Americans in favor of allowing doctors to hasten a terminally ill patient's death when the matter is described as allowing doctors to 'end the patient's life by some painless means.' At the same time, far fewer—51 percent—support it when the process is described as doctors helping a patient 'commit suicide.'" As was the case with abortion before *Roe v. Wade* (and as will be the case if *Roe* is overruled), whether or not you have the right to die through assisted suicide will, for the foreseeable future, depend on where you live.

16. The Right to Bear Arms

District of Columbia v. Heller (2008)
McDonald v. City of Chicago (2010)

Does the right to do what you want include the right to carry a handgun? Consider the arcane language of the Second Amendment: "A well regulated Militia, being necessary to the security of a free State, the right of the people to keep and bear Arms, shall not be infringed."

The Supreme Court's job is to determine what the Constitution means. Typically, that entails taking an understandable phrase and figuring out how it applies to a specific situation. For example, does criminalizing flag burning violate the First Amendment's prohibition against "abridging the freedom of speech"? Or does the practice of using a high-tech device placed outside a house to detect what might be going on inside violate the Fourth Amendment's prohibition against "unreasonable searches"? Or does the Constitution's guaranty of "equal protection" permit "separate but equal" treatment?

These are difficult, often tortuous issues. But in approaching these questions, the Supreme Court is at least dealing with comprehensible phraseology. We have a basic, shared understanding of the meaning of phrases like "abridging the freedom of speech," "unreasonable searches," and "equal protection." Individual justices may disagree on how to apply the words chosen by the framers of the Constitution to the circumstances of particular cases that come before the Court. But at least the justices start out on the same page, talking about basically the same generally understood concepts.

Not so with the Second Amendment, where, for decades, justices have disagreed over its basic meaning, as if they were debating the proper translation of an ancient text. The dispute centers on how the two clauses fit together. The first clause says that we need a "well regulated Militia." The second speaks of "the right of the people to keep and bear Arms." Does the first clause govern the second clause, such that the framers only intended to provide that the government cannot disarm citizens who are part of organized militias? Given the historical context, that interpretation makes sense. Just a few years earlier, groups of citizens formed their own militias, armed themselves with their own weapons, and helped to free the colonies from English rule. The framers most certainly understood that the best defense against a tyrannical government was an armed militia, and they would have wanted to prevent the new government from disarming the citizens who might find it necessary to join such militias in the future.

Or is the first clause just one example of why the right of the people to bear arms was so important to the framers? If the right were meant only to apply to people who served in militias, wouldn't the framers (classically educated men who most certainly knew how to express themselves) have said so? The second clause plainly references the right *of the people* to keep and bear Arms—not just the right of the people who serve in militias.

People often see what they want to see in the Second Amendment. Gun-control advocates argue that the first clause takes precedence, and that the Second Amendment grants only a militia-based collective right to bear arms. Gun-rights advocates argue that the reference to "the people" in the second clause means just what it says, and that the Second Amendment grants each individual, whether or not connected to a militia, the right to bear arms. It is among our most inflammatory issues. In many parts of the country, a candidate's stance on the Second Amendment will determine an election.

In 2008, the Supreme Court decided to reopen the question.

The Making of a Test Case

District of Columbia v. Heller was a classic test case, carefully constructed by organized and well-funded gun-rights advocates to focus on a narrow question: Does the Second Amendment provide an individual who is not affiliated with a militia the right to keep a gun in his home for purposes of self-defense? Their interest was in establishing that the Second Amendment was an *individual* right, not just the collective right of those in military service. Everything else having to do with what that right meant, how it might be limited, and in what other contexts it applied would await another day in court.

To raise that pristine question, they focused on the District of Columbia's gun ban, the nation's most extreme. The District had earned the unfortunate designation of the "murder capital of America," with the highest rate of firearms deaths per capita in the United States. In the hope of limiting the proliferation of firearms, the District effectively outlawed all handguns from homes, and required that rifles and shotguns could only be kept in homes if they were unloaded, disassembled, and bound by a trigger lock.

Those promoting the test case chose a group of citizens with diverse backgrounds to challenge the ban. For arcane legal reasons, only one, Dick Heller, remained to carry the issue by the time the case made it to the Supreme Court. Heller, a security guard with a spotless background who lived in the District, had tried to register a handgun that he wished to keep in his home for self-defense. Based solely on the District's gun ban, he was turned down.

Heller's position was simple. It removed all of the nuance and complexity, and framed the issue in a way the Supreme Court could not avoid. There was no question that Heller lived in an area where self-defense is a real concern. There was nothing about Heller himself that would justify denying him a handgun to be used for self-defense. All he asked for was the right to keep the kind of handgun in his home that is commonly used for self-defense. He raised no issue about his right to keep other kinds of guns, or to carry a gun outside of his home. The District's law gave him no other viable self-defense option—he could keep a rifle or shotgun in his home, but an armed intruder would not be likely to wait while he reassembled it and took off the trigger lock.

If, Heller argued to the Supreme Court, the Second Amendment gives individuals a constitutional right to own guns, then I have to win—I need a gun in my home for self-defense, I'm a sane and law-abiding adult, and there's no rational reason for the government to stop me. So just answer that one question for me, yes or no: Does the Second Amendment give me that right, or not?

Ideological Conservatives v. Ideological Liberals

The Court answered the question, and in doing so it split 5–4, along predictable, ideological lines—the Second Amendment retained its mirror-like ability to reflect what those who read it hope it says.

The so-called conservative wing of the Court (Justices Scalia, Thomas, Kennedy, Roberts, and Alito) won the day, and took the politically conservative position. Justice Antonin Scalia wrote the majority opinion, ultimately concluding that the right to bear arms is each individual's right, having nothing to do with service in a militia. "In sum," he wrote, "we hold that the District's ban on handgun posses-sion in the home violates the Second Amendment, as does its prohibi-tion against rendering any lawful firearm in the home operable for the purpose of immediate self-defense."

To reach that conclusion, Justice Scalia looked at the historical context in which the framers of the Constitution drafted the Second Amendment. The framers often used the term "the people," he reasoned, and when they did so they meant *all* the people, not just some subset, such as those who happened to be in militias. In the eighteenth century, unlike today, the militia was "the people," and the initial clause was not meant as a limitation on the right to bear arms. "Does the preface fit with an operative clause that creates an individual right to keep and bear arms?" Scalia asked. "It fits perfectly." Therefore, he ruled, the Second Amendment "surely elevates above all other interests the right of law-abiding, responsible citizens to use arms in defense of hearth and home." Gun possession may cause problems, he reasoned, but we cannot solve those problems through the violation of fundamental constitutional rights.

The so-called liberal wing of the Court (Justices Stevens, Souter, Ginsburg, and Breyer) took the politically liberal position and dissented. Justice John Paul Stevens wrote one of the dissents and, like Justice Scalia, he analyzed the historical context—and reached the opposite conclusion. He called Justice Scalia's interpretation of history "strained and unpersuasive." Justice Stevens argued that in addition to the focus on militias in the first clause, the phrase "to keep and bear arms" in the second clause was the kind of language that, at the time, pertained to military-like service. "The Court would have us believe that over 200 years ago, the Framers made a choice to limit the tools available to elected officials wishing to regulate civilian uses of weapons," he wrote. "I could not possibly conclude that the Framers made such a choice."

Typically, so-called conservatives respect precedent and criticize so-called liberals as being "activists" who too easily upset settled law to serve their own agendas. Here, Justice Stevens argued, it was the conservatives who were guilty of those judicial sins. "Until today, it has been understood that legislatures may regulate the civilian use and misuse of firearms so long as they do not interfere with the preservation of a well-regulated militia," Justice Stevens wrote in his dissent. "The

Court's announcement of a new constitutional right to own and use firearms for private purposes upsets that settled understanding."

So Much for Gun Bans.
What about Gun Controls?

Most modern constitutional scholars, even those who might call themselves political "liberals," seem to agree that despite its awkward syntax, the Second Amendment was meant to provide an individual right to bear arms, not just a collective right to do so within a militia. President Obama, for instance, a longtime constitutional law professor, agrees with this conclusion.

The real disagreement, however, centers on the issue of how far a town, a state, or the Congress can go in regulating that right.

Justice Stephen Breyer wrote a dissent in *Heller* in which he argued that even if there is an individual right to own a gun, it's not the same sort of right as free speech or freedom of religion. The law should allow an "interest-balancing approach" when it comes to firearms, he reasoned. We regulate all kinds of rights based on public safety (even free speech, as in the clichéd prohibition against yelling "Fire!" in a public theater), and if, as in the District of Columbia, there is a truly compelling need to ban firearms, the Second Amendment's right to bear arms should yield.

All of the liberals, and none of the conservatives, signed on to Justice Breyer's view. The conservatives saw the Second Amendment as something much more sacrosanct than Justice Breyer's view implied.

But at the same time, Justice Scalia's majority opinion made clear that some forms of gun-control regulation would be permissible. Yes, the Second Amendment provides a right to bear arms, Justice Scalia wrote, but it is "not a right to keep and carry any weapon whatsoever in any manner whatsoever and for whatever purpose." He took pains to point out that the decision "should [not] be taken to cast doubt" on the many forms of existing gun regulation. As Justice Stevens noted in his dissent, the *Heller* decision "leaves for future cases the formidable task of defining the scope" of future regulation on the right to bear arms.

McDonald v. City of Chicago: Closing the Circle

Right after *Heller* was decided, another lawsuit, *McDonald v. City of Chicago*, was filed in federal court in Chicago, challenging Chicago's stringent handgun laws.

Some background: As we have discussed, the United States is, of course, composed of a federal government and fifty state governments, each with a certain degree of autonomy. The Bill of Rights was specifically written to restrain the *federal* government from trampling on the rights of citizens and the various states, but it was by no means clear if, or how, the Bill of Rights applied to the states themselves. Long constitutional law story made very short: ultimately, the Supreme Court decided that those rights among the Bill of Rights that were *fundamental*, the core rights of Americans, applied to the states as well as the federal government.

McDonald was filed for one purpose: to obtain a ruling from the Supreme Court that the Second Amendment rights as defined and endorsed by *Heller were* fundamental rights that applied to the states (and the municipalities in the states).

Here is how Justice Alito, writing for the 5–4 majority in *McDonald*, put it: "[W]e must decide whether the right to keep and bear arms is fundamental to our scheme of ordered liberty, or as we have said in a related context, whether this right is 'deeply rooted in this Nation's history and tradition.'"

Another long constitutional law story made very short (the various *McDonald* opinions exceed two hundred pages), here is how Justice Alito framed his conclusion in the majority opinion: "Our decision in *Heller* points unmistakably to the answer. Self-defense is a basic right, recognized by many legal systems from ancient times to the present day. . . . *Heller* makes it clear that this right is 'deeply rooted in this Nation's history and tradition.'"

Justice Breyer, writing on behalf of a defeated minority, disagreed: "In sum, the Framers did not write the Second Amendment in order to protect a private right of armed self defense. There has been, and is, no consensus that the right is, or was, 'fundamental.'"

The Future: A Shot in the Dark . . .

McDonald is as important for what it says as for what it does *not* say. The *McDonald* Court said that, yes, the Second Amendment *does* apply to the states—but we are going to leave the question of how and to what extent it applies for another day. Justice Alito acknowledged that, consequently, the *McDonald* decision would "lead to extensive and costly litigation" as lawsuit after lawsuit was brought to flesh out the scope of permissible regulation but, he said, that was the price of protecting constitutional freedoms. Justice Stevens thought that approach was cavalier and risky, warning that the ruling "invites an avalanche of litigation that could mire the federal courts in fine-grained determinations about which state and local regulations comport with the *Heller* right—the precise contours of which are far from pellucid—under a standard of review we have not even established."

So, while the combined force of the *Heller* and *McDonald* decisions defined the outlines of a very important painting, they left the details of the painting for another time. These details will be completed by future courts in future cases, through the same exquisite ballet that has shaped our rights of free speech, our religious rights, our rights to be free from unreasonable searches, our rights of equal protection and due process, and all of the other rights that define so much of America. Court challenges to existing and newly formulated regulations will be filed; lower courts will make decisions; the Supreme Court will review some of those decisions; and new lines will be drawn.

The end product of these efforts will, like so many of the Roberts Court 5–4 decisions we have discussed, depend on the predilections of those who sit on the Supreme Court in the future. In the meantime, there will be uncertainty, which is one of the prices to be paid in a democracy where, thankfully, the law evolves through a participatory and deliberative—often political—process. Not perfect, but consider the alternatives.

17. The Constitutional Right to Marry

Obergefell et al. v. Hodges (2014)

Obergefell v. Hodges established the right—the *constitutional* right—of same-sex couples to marry. But the case is just as important and intriguing for other reasons, as reflected in four startlingly vituperative dissents that do not question whether same-sex marriage should be lawful so much as they question the role and authority of the Supreme Court in our system of government. *Obergefell* illuminates the constitutional tensions between the states and the federal government, and it demonstrates how the Supreme Court, and the meaning of the Constitution itself, is profoundly, and seemingly inevitably, influenced by changes in culture and public opinion despite the protests of those who (depending on the context) argue that the Constitution loses all force and power—that we risk becoming a government of men and not laws—if it is interpreted (and re-interpreted) based on those changes.

The Backstory

Like so many Supreme Court cases, *Obergefell* began with an individual who thought he was right and that government officials were wrong. On that level, the case is yet another demonstration of the power our constitutional system affords the individual to confront, and defeat, the government.

James Obergefell met John Arthur when they were in their twenties. They fell in love and began a long-term committed relationship. In 2011, Arthur was diagnosed with ALS, an incurable neurological disease. Two years later, as Arthur's disease progressed to the point where he was bedridden, Obergefell and Arthur decided to marry, but they lived in Ohio, where same-sex marriage was unlawful.

Obergefell placed a post on Facebook seeking help and advice—and within a short time, friends and family raised the $13,000 needed to charter a medical jet to fly Obergefell and Arthur to Maryland, where same-sex marriage was legal. Arthur's condition had progressed to the point where it was very difficult for him to move, and they married inside the plane, Arthur in a hospital bed, on the tarmac of the Baltimore airport.

After they returned home to Cincinnati, Obergefell and Arthur consulted counsel, and learned that, under Ohio law, even though they had been legally married in Maryland, when Arthur died, his death certificate would not list Obergefell as his spouse—and in July 2013, they decided to file suit, seeking a court order requiring the spousal designation. Arthur died three months later, and Obergefell resolved to continue the fight. He was joined by other plaintiffs who asserted their own rights to have their same-sex marriages recognized, and by a funeral director who sought the right to reflect a lawful same-sex marriage on the death certificates he was responsible to complete.

Obergefell contended that, under the Constitution, Ohio was required to recognize a same-sex marriage performed in a state where same-sex marriages were legal. In December 2013, Obergefell and the other plaintiffs won the first round. Ohio appealed, and the appeals court reversed the lower court in November 2014. Shortly thereafter, the Supreme Court agreed to hear the case.

The Battlefield: Rights and Fundamental Rights

The Constitution created the federal government but, at the same time, the drafters were extremely wary of what they created. They recognized the need to unify the colonies for many, but not all, purposes, and they wanted to make sure that the lines of authority were clearly drawn—which is why the last enumerated right in the Bill of Rights states that "The powers not delegated to the United States by the Constitution, nor prohibited by it to the states, are reserved to the states respectively, or to the people." In other words, unless the Constitution says the federal government can, it can't.

But, of course, that still leaves open the obvious question: What does the Constitution say about what the federal government is empowered to do?

In cases like *Obergefell*, involving an individual who wants to do something a state or the federal government says the individual cannot do, that question boils down to the meaning of two monumentally important provisions in the Fourteenth Amendment to the Constitution: the Due Process Clause (no person shall be "deprived of life, liberty, or property without due process of law"); and the "Equal Protection Clause" (no state shall deny to any person within its jurisdiction "the equal protection of the laws"). As interpreted over decades by the Supreme Court, the Due Process Clause is intended to protect persons from governmental interference with the fundamental rights associated with life, liberty, or property, and the Equal Protection Clause is intended to ensure that the government does not arbitrarily afford the benefits of these fundamental rights to some persons but not others. The word "fundamental" is the key. The Constitution does not guaranty due process and equal protection respecting all rights; it applies to *fundamental* rights, and in respect to everything else, the states are free to govern as they think best.

But what rights are "fundamental" rights? That issue is a crucial battlefield on which the schools of constitutional interpretation wage their wars. Should the Court define the undefined terms in the Constitution (like "due process" and "equal protection") broadly, based on changing times? Should the Court try to divine the intentions and philosophies of the drafters? Should the Court read the words as they were defined when written and stop there?

These differences are passionately, and sometimes bitterly, fought over. The constitutional stakes are as high as they get. What rights does the federal government protect? To what extent will the federal government define our lives? *Obergefell* provided an arena in which the justices fought these issues to the philosophical death.

Did the Supreme Court Protect a Constitutional Right? Or Did It Make Policy?

This was another decision where, predictably, the four so-called liberals and the four so-called conservatives formed their blocs, with Justice Kennedy in the middle. This time, unlike *Citizens United*, for instance, Justice Kennedy sided with the liberals, and he wrote the majority opinion: he found that same-sex marriage *is* a fundamental right protected by the Due Process and Equal Protection Clauses of the Constitution.

Justice Kennedy's rationale was that the liberties guaranteed by the Bill of Rights "extend to certain personal choices central to individual dignity and autonomy, including intimate choices that define personal identity and beliefs." He extolled the institution of marriage and its importance to society, and concluded that all persons have the constitutional right to the legal, as well as the personal, benefits a marriage provides. The hope of same-sex couples, he said, "is not to be condemned to live in loneliness, excluded from one of civilization's oldest institutions. They ask for equal dignity in the eyes of the law. The Constitution grants them that right."

Justice Kennedy anticipated the dissenters' argument that nothing in the Constitution, the intent of the drafters, or Supreme Court precedent supports the notion that the right to marry is a fundamental right that demands constitutional protection. His answer: "The generations that wrote and ratified the Bill of Rights and the Fourteenth Amendment did not presume to know the extent of freedom in all of its dimensions, and so they entrusted to future generations a charter protecting the right of all persons to enjoy liberty as we learn its meaning." In other words, the Constitution is a living document that the drafters intended to evolve as society evolved.

Why not leave the question to the states, which have traditionally dealt with the legalities of marriage? Justice Kennedy's view was that it would be unconstitutional to make same-sex couples wait for state legislatures to recognize what was to Justice Kennedy a clear right that had to be respected without delay. "The dynamic of our constitutional system is that individuals need not await legislative action before asserting a fundamental right."

Reflecting their level of outrage, each of the four dissenting justices wrote a scathing dissent, as if they each wanted history to know the extent to which they disagreed with what the majority had done. In general, they each struck the same chords: the majority had stepped over a sacrosanct line that separates the judiciary from the legislature in order to impose a preferred policy that had no basis in constitutional law.

Justice Scalia seethed. Justice Kennedy and the four justices who agreed with him, Scalia wrote, "have discovered in the Fourteenth Amendment a 'fundamental right' overlooked by every person alive at the time of ratification, and almost everyone else in the time since." In vintage Justice Scalia fashion, he continued:

> The majority's decision is an act of will, not legal judgment. The right it announces has no basis in the Constitution or this Court's precedent. The majority expressly disclaims judicial "caution" and omits even a pretense of humility, openly relying on its desire to remake society according to its own "new insight" into the "nature of injustice." . . . As a result, the Court invalidates the marriage laws of more than half the States and orders the

transformation of a social institution that has formed the basis of human society for millennia, for the Kalahari Bushmen and the Han Chinese, the Carthaginians and the Aztecs. Just who do we think we are?

Chief Justice Roberts emphatically underlined the point. "Stripped of its shiny rhetorical gloss, the majority's argument is that the Due Process Clause gives same-sex couples a fundamental right to marry because it will be good for them and for society. If I were a legislator, I would certainly consider that view as a matter of social policy. But as a judge, I find the majority's position indefensible as a matter of constitutional law."

Justice Scalia went even further. "A system of government that makes the People subordinate to a committee of nine unelected lawyers does not deserve to be called a democracy."

What Does the Future Hold?

Some have prognosticated that *Obergefell* may signal the advent of a Court that will more expansively define the Due Process and Equal Protection clauses in a way that will further enlarge the reach of the Constitution into matters typically reserved for the states. As discussed in the note to the 2nd Revised & Updated Edition, however, that remains pure speculation until the future alignment of the Court is determined over the next several years. But whether one agrees or disagrees with the approach taken and the decision made by Justices Kennedy, Breyer, Ginsburg, Kagan, and Sotomayor, *Obergefell* highlights how momentously important the selection of the next one or two justices will be to the practical meaning of due process and equal protection—and that will likely determine the point at which constitutional law and the everyday lives of Americans (and others) will intersect, for at least the next generation.

Thirty-ninth Congress of the United States at the first Session, begun and held at the City of Washington, in the District of Columbia, on Monday, the fourth day of December, one thousand eight hundred and sixty-five.

Joint Resolution proposing an amendment to the Constitution of the United States.

Be it resolved by the Senate and House of Representatives of the United States of America in Congress assembled, (two-thirds of both Houses concurring,) That the following article be proposed to the legislatures of the several States as an amendment to the Constitution of the United States, which, when ratified by three-fourths of said legislatures, shall be valid as part of the Constitution, namely:

Article XIV.

Section 1. All persons born or naturalized in the United States, and subject to the jurisdiction thereof, are citizens of the United States and of the State wherein they reside. No State shall make or enforce any law which shall abridge the privileges or immunities of citizens of the United States; nor shall any State deprive any person of life, liberty, or property, without due process of law, nor deny to any person within its jurisdiction the equal protection of the laws.

Section 2. Representatives shall be apportioned among the several States according to their respective numbers, counting the whole number of persons in each State, excluding Indians not taxed. But when the right to vote at any election for the choice of electors for President and Vice President of the United States, Representatives in Congress, the Executive and Judicial officers of a State, or the members of the Legislature thereof, is denied to any of the male inhabitants of such State, being twenty-one years of age, and citizens of the United States, or in any way abridged, except for participation in rebellion, or other crime, the basis of representation therein shall be reduced in the proportion which the

CHAPTER 7

"BIG GOVERNMENT" IN YOUR BUSINESS AND YOUR BACKYARD

*"Liberty implies the absence of arbitrary restraint,
not immunity from reasonable regulations . . ."*

—CHARLES EVANS HUGHES, SUPREME COURT JUSTICE, 1930–41

The venerated Due Process Clause of the Fourteenth Amendment prohibits the government from depriving any person "of life, liberty, or property, without due process of law." Stated differently, the government can take your property, your liberty, and even your life, so long as it goes about doing it in the right way.

This principle applies in a myriad of contexts, one of which is the world of commerce: just how far can the government go in restricting how people conduct business, or in regulating what happens on the job, or in deciding who wins the conflicts between business interests and individual rights?

The answer to these questions can be complex, implicating not only the Due Process Clause, but other constitutional provisions as well. Decades ago, the Supreme Court seemingly defined much of this legal landscape but, as will be seen, it may now be in the process of changing its mind in important ways, and where it ultimately ends up will have profound effects on the role of government in our society.

A detail of page one of the Fourteenth Amendment.

18. What Gives Congress the Right to Regulate Private Businesses?

West Coast Hotel Co. v. Parrish (1937)

In the early 1900s, state legislatures began to enact measures designed to protect workers, such as child labor laws, maximum-hour laws, and workers' compensation laws. The Supreme Court, however, quickly put the constitutional brakes on these efforts, setting the stage for a momentous power struggle and constitutional crisis decades later. The outcome of that struggle would determine not only whether Congress would be permitted to protect workers, but also whether it would be permitted to address the country's social issues, ranging from outlawing segregation to protecting the food supply.

The conflict began in earnest when New York enacted a law limiting the work week to a maximum of sixty hours in certain industries. The law was challenged, and in 1905 the case, *Lochner v. New York*, worked its way to the Supreme Court. The Court's analysis in *Lochner* focused on the Due Process Clause of the Fourteenth Amendment to the Constitution: "No person shall be . . . deprived of life, liberty, or property, without due process of law." Central to this right, said the Court, was the liberty to enter into contracts without government interference, and that included contracts between employers and employees. Based on that logic, in a 5–4 decision the Court ruled that laws "limiting the hours in which grown and intelligent men may labor to earn their living" are "mere meddlesome interferences with the rights of the individual." The New York law was ruled unconstitutional. In effect, the Supreme Court ruled that the government was obligated to leave businesses, and the people who worked for and dealt with businesses, to their own devices.

Roosevelt's Reaction:
The "Court-Packing Plan"

Lochner remained unchallenged until Franklin D. Roosevelt and the "New Dealers" took power in the wake of the Great Depression. A fundamental part of Roosevelt's economic recovery plan was the implementation of health and safety codes. Court challenges to these codes predictably resulted, and in 1935, using the *Lochner* precedent, the Supreme Court began to dismantle what Roosevelt had done: It invalidated an act that allowed farmers to hold onto their farms during foreclosure; it invalidated minimum wage, maximum hour, and health codes in the poultry industry; and it invalidated Roosevelt's key agricultural reforms.

Roosevelt was beyond livid, and on February 5, 1937, he unveiled what came to be known as the "court-packing plan": Roosevelt sought to cajole Congress into passing a law that would allow him to appoint an extra Supreme Court justice for each present justice who was over seventy, which, at that time, would have increased the number of justices from nine to sixteen. Roosevelt's ostensible purpose was to assist older justices to carry the Court's workload, but his obvious intent was to gain control over a Court that he viewed as a dangerous impediment to economic recovery and social justice. Roosevelt lobbied hard for the legislation through vituperative attacks on the Court, back-room deal-making, and nationally broadcast "fireside chats." While there was support for the plan in some quarters, there was substantial suspicion as well—if the president could, essentially, "rig" the Court to suit his purposes, what would become of the "check and balance" role the Supreme Court was to play in the Constitution's elegant plan?

Less than two months later, while Senate hearings on Roosevelt's plan were proceeding, the Supreme Court handed down a decision in the case of *West Coast Hotel Co. v. Parrish*. The case involved a challenge to the constitutionality of the state of Washington's minimum-wage laws. The Supreme Court had recently overturned similar laws by a 5–4 margin, and it was expected that the *West Coast Hotel* case would face the same fate.

The Switch in Time That Saved Nine

This time, however, the 5–4 majority went the other way—one of the justices, Justice Owen J. Roberts, inexplicably switched his vote and signed on to an opinion authored by Chief Justice Charles Evans Hughes, who abandoned *Lochner* in favor of a rationale that became the foundation for national minimum-wage laws, Social Security, the regulation of public utilities, agricultural quotas, and much more. Liberty, said the chief justice (along with his newfound colleague), be it freedom of contract or any other liberty, is not absolute, but can and must be regulated so that the citizenry may be protected against "the evils which menace the health, safety, morals, and welfare of the people."

This was sweet music to FDR's ears, and the confrontation between the executive and the judiciary quickly became a collaboration. Justice Roberts's change of heart was soon dubbed the "switch in time that saved nine." Historians have never been able to definitively establish whether Justice Roberts's turnabout was the result of the pressure exerted by Roosevelt on the Court or an honest change in viewpoint, but, in the years that followed, Roosevelt was able to implement the social legislation of the New Deal without further interference from the Supreme Court, and the congressional impetus to keep enacting such legislation continued for more than fifty years.

19. What Are the Limits on Congress's Right to Regulate Business, and Beyond?

Heart of Atlanta Motel v. United States (1964)
Katzenbach v. McClung (1964)

The *West Coast Hotel* case cleared the way for Congress, whether on its own or at the urging of the president, to enact broad-brush business legislation that changed the way Americans live. But the decision raised two far-reaching questions.

First, does the federal government's right to regulate business stop at the national or, at worst, the industry level? Or can it also reach into local communities and regulate individual businesses? For instance, can the federal government dictate how much the corner store must pay its employees, or what hours it can operate? Or should issues like those be decided strictly on the community or, at worst, the state level?

Second, if the federal government is ultimately allowed to reach into local towns in order to tell businesses how to behave, is it also allowed to dictate what subjects must be taught in the local schools, and who the local police department is permitted to hire? Where does the power stop?

Much of the answer lies in a provision in the Constitution known as the "Commerce Clause," and the extent of the power that provision gives the federal government is now the subject of one of the hottest Supreme Court debates in decades. Two cases decided in the 1960s, *Heart of Atlanta Motel v. United States* and *Katzenbach v. McClung*, took the pendulum about as far as it could go in one direction, but it now appears to be quickly swinging the other way.

Some background is necessary to understand how we got where we are and where we may be going.

The Supreme Court Expands the Commerce Clause

In the years before the Constitution was created, the states had been waging economic wars among themselves through protective tariffs and retaliatory trade regulations, making the creation of a national economy virtually impossible. This was one of the major reasons why the Founding Fathers convened a Constitutional Convention—the goal was to forge a federal government with sufficient power to create a workable system of national commerce. The so-called Commerce Clause of the Constitution was the result: It granted Congress the power "to Regulate Commerce with foreign nations, and among the Several States, and with the Indian Tribes."

In the early nineteenth century, Congress began to flex its federal muscles, and it enacted a variety of laws requiring that the states cease interference with interstate commerce so that a national economy might develop more quickly. For instance, it imposed interstate rail and shipping rates and practices so that one state could not, through its own laws, obtain an economic leg up on another state. When these laws were challenged as being beyond congressional authority, the Supreme Court ruled that, in fact, Congress had been empowered by the Commerce Clause to regulate interstate commerce, and it therefore had the right under the Constitution to take such actions.

Through the remainder of the nineteenth century and into the twentieth century, as industry expanded and the economy grew, Congress further amplified its legislative activities, and the businesses that bore the brunt of these regulations again challenged them in court. Often, the challenge was based on the fact that the activity Congress sought to regulate took place within just one state, as opposed to taking place in "interstate commerce." For instance, Congress passed laws regulating what occurred in stockyards, even though each stockyard was situated in only a single state.

The Supreme Court allowed these laws to stand, by dramatically expanding the concept of "interstate commerce" to include economic activities that took place solely within one state, on the theory that such activities plainly affected commerce in other states. For example, it ruled that a stockyard located and doing business only in Chicago could nonetheless be regulated by Congress because the livestock in the stockyard were ultimately destined for shipment to states all over the country—that is, the stockyard was connected to an interstate distribution chain and was therefore itself in interstate commerce. Using this interpretation of "interstate commerce," the Court allowed Congress to implement legislation imposing workplace rules, establishing union rights, mandating payment for overtime, setting commodity prices, regulating strip mining, and controlling a host of other in-state economic activities, all on the theory that the activities "affected" interstate commerce, and were therefore authorized by the Commerce Clause.

Taking the Commerce Clause to, and Perhaps Beyond, the Limit

The Supreme Court's willingness to expand Congress's rights under the Commerce Clause reached a zenith in 1964. Congress passed the Civil Rights Act of 1964 to prohibit discrimination on the basis of race, color, religion, or national origin in places of public accommodation, like hotels and restaurants. Congress knew that its right to regulate private conduct of this type was questionable—the Civil Rights Act did not really focus on regulating economic activity in the same way that legislation affecting, for instance, stockyards and commodities did. It was plainly focused on ending discrimination, and nothing more. However, Congress inserted a provision stating that a facility was covered under the Act "if its operations affect commerce"; Congress hoped that the

Supreme Court would use that language as a hook to rule that the Commerce Clause gave Congress the power it needed to do just about anything Congress wanted to do.

As expected, the Civil Rights Act of 1964 was immediately challenged in court. The Heart of Atlanta Motel, located in downtown Atlanta, insisted on continuing its practice of refusing to rent rooms to blacks. The motel was near a highway and served intrastate as well as interstate travelers. Similarly, Ollie's Barbecue, a large restaurant in Birmingham, Alabama, insisted on continuing its practice of serving whites at tables, but providing only takeout service for blacks. It purchased some of its food—approximately $70,000 a year—from out-of-state suppliers, and served interstate travelers. The owners of both establishments argued that the Commerce Clause could not logically be used to give the federal government regulatory power over their businesses, which had only microscopic and indirect effects on interstate commerce.

The cases that resulted from these court challenges, *Heart of Atlanta Motel v. United States* and *Katzenbach v. McClung*, ultimately reached the Supreme Court—and in deciding those cases, the Court upheld the power of Congress to enact the Civil Rights Act of 1964 pursuant to the authority granted by the Commerce Clause. These decisions were monumentally important: For better or worse, they validated Congress's right not only to fight racial discrimination throughout the country, but to reach into local towns and attack virtually all manner of social ills and wrongs through federal lawmaking. The body of social legislation that arose from Congress during the 1960s, 1970s, and 1980s can in large measure be attributed to these decisions.

The rationale the Court used in the *Heart of Atlanta Motel* and *Katzenbach* cases stretched the words of the Commerce Clause to (and some say beyond) their limits. The Court reasoned that both businesses, even though they did not directly engage in interstate commerce, catered to people who themselves moved in interstate commerce, and it stood to reason that the cumulative effect of discriminating against a portion of those people affected interstate commerce in some substantial way. It was not necessary, said the Court, to engage in quantification efforts or detailed analyses—if it could be rationally concluded that the activities Congress was regulating had a material effect on interstate commerce, that was enough.

The Supreme Court's Retreat

Based on these Commerce Clause precedents, there was little that was beyond Congress's reach—and Congress took full advantage of its power, enacting federal legislation that affected innumerable aspects of local life. Critics complained that this distorted the Commerce Clause beyond its plain meaning and gave Congress powers the Founding Fathers had never intended it to have.

By 1995, however, a majority of the Supreme Court was composed of justices who shared these critics' judicial philosophies, and the result has been a serious change in direction, with major implications.

It began with the 1995 case of *United States v. Lopez*. The Supreme Court addressed the constitutionality of the Gun-Free School Zones Act of 1990, in which Congress made it a federal offense for a person to possess a firearm in a school zone. The Act was challenged in court, and, in a 5–4 decision handed down in 1995, the Supreme Court ruled that the regulation of guns in school zones did not involve a sufficient connection to economic activity to implicate the federal government's Commerce Clause powers, and the federal government was therefore legislating in a realm in which it had no authority. The decision floored most legal analysts, who had come to take the Commerce Clause for granted.

Five years later, in 2000, the Supreme Court did it again. In the case of *United States v. Morrison*, the Court faced a challenge to a federal law that prohibited violence against women. In another 5–4 decision, the Supreme Court ruled that the law exceeded the federal government's power under the Commerce Clause. Even though violence against women may have economic implications that affect interstate commerce, the Court ruled that "crimes of violence are not, in any sense of the phrase, economic activity" and Congress was therefore not empowered under the Commerce Clause to legislate in that arena. *Lopez* was no longer an aberration; it appeared to be part of a trend.

In both cases, the four dissenting justices fervently pointed out that Congress had assembled evidence in reports and hearings establishing that violence in schools substantially affects the quality of education, and a lesser-educated workforce has an obvious effect on interstate commerce. Even more troubling, they reasoned, Congress had established a "mountain of data" assembled during four years of hearings documenting the substantial effects that violence against women has on the economy—far more than any evidence that supported the decisions in the *Heart of Atlanta Motel* and *Katzenbach* cases. The majority was unmoved.

The Challenge to "Obamacare"

In 2012, the trend continued, in *National Federation of Independent Businesses v. Sebelius*. In 2010, Congress passed the Affordable Care Act, the signature legislation of the Obama administration. The heart and financial foundation of the Affordable Care Act was the "individual mandate"—the requirement that nearly all individuals maintain minimum health insurance coverage or pay a penalty to the IRS. Thirteen states filed a lawsuit claiming (among other things) that the individual mandate violated the Commerce Clause and was therefore unconstitutional. If the Supreme Court agreed, the Affordable Care Act would, for all practical purposes, be nullified, and the political and practical fallout would be monumental.

Many Court "insiders" have written that Chief Justice Roberts, concerned over the Roberts Court's legacy and the tumult that would result from invalidating the Affordable Care Act, struggled to find a way to preserve the Act while, at the same time, supporting the position of those who sought to limit the reach of the Commerce Clause—and that is exactly what Chief Justice Roberts did.

An *extremely* unlikely alliance was formed: Chief Justice Roberts joined with the "liberal" wing of the Court: Justices Ginsburg, Breyer, Sotomayor, and Kagan. Chief Justice Roberts then wrote a 5–4 opinion in which he had his cake and ate it too. Navigating an array of legal twists and turns, he *upheld* the individual mandate as a valid exercise of Congress's power to tax (an act of "verbal wizardry," wrote the dissenters), but also concluded that the individual mandate violated the Commerce Clause because the "Federal Government does not have the power to order people to buy health insurance." Even though "Obamacare" remained in effect, the dilution of the federal government's Commerce Clause authority remained a central theme of the Supreme Court's "conservative" bloc.

These cases, and the whole idea of the Commerce Clause, may seem somewhat esoteric, but they raise a fundamental issue: What is the role of the federal government in solving the country's social problems? The law is plainly in flux, particularly after the passing of Justice Scalia, but at least four of the current justices appear to be bent on transferring a substantial degree of responsibility for social problems from the Capitol to the statehouses and the town halls.

20. Expanding the Right of Employees to Sue Their Employers

Burlington Industries v. Ellerth (1998)

Sometimes it is the Supreme Court itself, not Congress, that multiplies the scope and effect of government regulation. Such was the case in the 1998 case of *Burlington Industries v. Ellerth*, where the Supreme Court, acting in the role of interpreting an Act of Congress, changed the rules of the American workplace and made it much easier for employees to win sexual-harassment and other lawsuits against their employers. The result has been a major increase in employee-versus-employer lawsuits, many ending in six- and seven-figure verdicts, and a radical shift in the way employers must manage their workforces.

Ellerth, a Burlington Industries salesperson, was subjected to constant sexual harassment from her supervisor. However, even though she knew that Burlington prohibited sexual harassment, she did not report her supervisor's misconduct, and she eventually quit. Ellerth then sued Burlington, claiming that the sexual harassment had forced her to resign.

At the trial, Burlington proved that it had done all anyone could have reasonably expected it to do. It had established clear policies forbidding sexual harassment; it did not know about the sexual harassment that Ellerth had suffered; and, absent a report from Ellerth, it had no realistic way of finding out about it. Burlington's defense was airtight: it was not negligent, and, as a result, it should not be held liable for the unknown acts of a renegade supervisor who was furtively violating Burlington's policies. Burlington won the case in the trial court.

Ellerth filed an appeal, and ultimately the Supreme Court agreed to hear her case. Ellerth contended that the Supreme Court should change the law of sexual harassment by applying a legal doctrine well entrenched in other kinds of cases, known as "vicarious liability." If, for instance, a company's truck driver runs a red light and causes an accident, the law provides that the company is "vicariously liable" for the actions of its employee, whether or not the company was itself negligent. The same would be true if, for instance, a nurse working for a group of doctors negligently injured a patient, or if a waiter working for a restaurant dropped a tray on a customer. In each case, the employer would be vicariously liable for the actions of its employee, even though the employer itself had done nothing wrong.

Why, asked Ellerth, shouldn't Burlington be vicariously liable for what its supervisor did to her, even if Burlington itself was not directly at fault?

Ellerth won—with some complications. The *Ellerth* case boiled down to two crucial rulings, each of which comprises a sea change in the law of the workplace.

First, the Supreme Court ruled that in cases where a supervisor sexually harasses an employee, and in the process takes some negative action against the employee (such as denying a raise or promotion), the company will be held liable, no matter what, even if the company actively prohibited sexual harassment, never knew that the sexual harassment was taking place, and did nothing else wrong.

Second, the Supreme Court ruled that even when no negative action is taken against the employee, if the employee is made to work in a sexually suggestive atmosphere that is unreasonably offensive— what the courts call a "hostile work environment"—the employer will be held liable, unless it can prove that it did all it reasonably could to prevent and correct the harassment and that the employee failed to take advantage of preventive or corrective opportunities the employer provided.

The Workplace, Reworked

Since the *Ellerth* decision was rendered, its directives have been expanded beyond the sexual harassment context and into related areas such as employee allegations of harassment or discrimination based on race, nationality, and religion. Old rule: an employer is not liable for a supervisor's unlawful treatment of an employee unless the employer is at fault by, for instance, knowingly permitting a renegade supervisor to remain on the job. New rule: Employers must proactively train and police their supervisors as part of a program to prevent unlawful conduct *before* it happens and must aggressively address all allegations of unlawful conduct as soon as they surface—if they do not, they risk an avalanche of lawsuits to which they may have no defense.

The upshot of *Ellerth* has been a massive shift in the balance of power between employees and their employers. As so often happens, this change in legal fundamentals fomented a change in societal fundamentals. The amplified risk of employee claims created, as a matter of financial necessity, the need for employers to mandate new standards of conduct not only between management and employees, but among employees themselves.

Post-*Ellerth* decisions have resulted in some pro-employer rulings. For example, in 2013, in *Vance v. Ball State University*, the Supreme Court overruled the Equal Employment Opportunity Commission's efforts to define "supervisor" to include anyone with the power to direct an employee's daily activities (like, perhaps, a senior coworker or working foreman). Instead, in a victory for employers, the Court ruled that for purposes of applying *Ellerth*, a supervisor must have the power to effectuate "tangible employment changes," like hiring, firing, promotions, and wage changes. Also in 2013, in *University of Texas Southwestern Medical Center v. Nassar*, the Court clarified the high burden of proof employees must satisfy in order to prevail on retaliation claims—that is, claims in which employees charge that their employers retaliated against them for complaining about unlawful workplace discrimination.

These cases did not limit *Ellerth* as much as they prevented the further expansion of *Ellerth*, and the decision's legacy is clear and entrenched: *Ellerth*'s transformation of the employer-employee rules of engagement has markedly changed the interactions and economics of the American workplace.

21. Eliminating Monopolies and Price-Fixing: John D. Rockefeller and the Birth of the Antitrust Laws

Standard Oil Co. v. United States (1911)

Think what things would be like if there were only one or two cell-phone providers, pharmaceutical firms, or automobile companies. As things stand, you cannot watch television or read a magazine without being deluged with advertisements touting the superiority of one brand over another, and the price wars among competing companies can be fierce. But if there were only one or two companies in these fields, the incentive to innovate new and better products at cheaper prices would not be nearly as intense—and the consumer would suffer. Competition has always been viewed as a key to the free enterprise system.

"Antitrust law" is designed to preserve competition. The basic statutes were enacted by Congress in the late 1800s and early 1900s, but it was the Supreme Court that put flesh on the statutory bones, beginning in 1911 with the *Standard Oil Co. v. United States* case.

Restraints of Trade and the "Rule of Reason"

The Standard Oil Company was founded by John D. Rockefeller. Through a combination of ruthlessness and creativity, Rockefeller managed to combine the vast majority of the country's oil refining and distribution capacities under one roof, creating a classic monopoly. Having eliminated the competition, he could sell and charge what he wanted to whomever he wanted, and he did.

Spurred by muckraking journalists, the government ultimately took action and brought suit, under the relatively new Sherman Antitrust

Act, to break up Standard Oil into separate competitive businesses. The trial consumed weeks (the record includes some 14,000 pages of testimony), and the Supreme Court eventually agreed to render the final ruling.

In an undeniably landmark case, the Court broke up Standard Oil into separate geographic units (not unlike what happened in the telephone industry decades later). In so doing, the Court announced a new rule to be applied in future monopoly cases—the so-called "rule of reason." The Sherman Act had prohibited any "restraint of trade," but the Supreme Court decided that only "unreasonable" restraints of trade (of which Standard Oil was the poster child) would be unlawful. In so doing, the Supreme Court gave birth to the federal government's power to analyze and, if warranted, seek the breakup of companies (as it attempted to do to Microsoft) and to minutely review and, if warranted, disallow proposed mergers that might restrain competition.

Price-Fixing and "Per Se" Violations

Ever creative, companies in the early 1900s pursued another activity that allowed them to raise prices without creating monopolies: price-fixing agreements. The leaders of competing companies in an industry would simply agree among themselves to maintain prices at an agreed-upon level, rather than trying to undercut one another. The usual effects of competition would be blunted, and the consumer would suffer.

Building on the *Standard Oil* precedent, in 1927, in the case of *United States v. Trenton Potteries Co.*, the Supreme Court ruled that price-fixing agreements among competitors are by definition an unreasonable restraint of trade, whether or not the levels at which prices were fixed were or were not reasonable. This became known as a "per se" violation of the antitrust laws, meaning that simply doing it is against the law, without regard for any "rule of reason." In the intervening decades, various other forms of collusion among ostensible competitors have been identified as per se violations as well.

Antitrust law has evolved into a huge body of court decisions, statutes, and regulations that permit both enforcement actions by the government and suits by private citizens and companies for antitrust violations. Scholarly debates among economists and politicians pertaining to the economic policies that should underlie the enforcement of the antitrust laws are ongoing, leading to different approaches taken by different administrations and different courts at different times. But when all is said and done, in the Standard Oil case the Supreme Court set forth the basics of some of the most important rules by which corporate America must live.

22. Can the Government Take Your House to Promote a Private Business?

Kelo v. City of New London (2005)

The concept of the government taking your house because it wants to use your property for some other purpose is frightening to contemplate. However, even before the Constitution was drafted in 1787, it was a given that a sovereign nation had this power of "eminent domain" or "condemnation." Our Founding Fathers recognized this in the Fifth Amendment to the Constitution, but restricted the right of the government to take private property (upon payment of just compensation) to one purpose: "public use."

Most citizens understand this as a necessary but limited evil that allows the government to take private property only in very rare circumstances, such as when a house lies in the path of a needed highway that will be used by the general public, or for a water-treatment plant or similar public facility. Taking someone's home is not something a democracy that respects individual rights does unless absolutely necessary.

But can private property be lawfully taken in order to promote private business interests?

A Castle No More?

In 1997, Susette Kelo purchased and restored a home with a river view in the Fort Trumbull neighborhood in New London, Connecticut. Many other families lived in this older middle-class neighborhood as well; some had been there for many generations.

New London's economy had been faltering for some time and, in 1998, the pharmaceutical company Pfizer began building a major research facility next to the Fort Trumbull neighborhood. New London saw this as an opportunity for economic development and revitalization and, through a private development agency controlled by city government, it developed a plan to create jobs and increase tax revenues. The plan called for the purchase and demolition of the Fort Trumbull houses, after which private developers would build a resort hotel and conference center, research facilities, new homes, offices, and retail space where the Fort Trumbull houses had formerly stood.

New London began making deals to buy the properties in Fort Trumbull (there were 115 separate lots) for this purpose. When all was said and done, the owners of fifteen lots, including Kelo, refused to sell. New London then commenced eminent domain proceedings in order to force the holdouts to sell their properties. In response, Kelo and the other holdouts sued to protect their homes, claiming that the proceedings would violate their constitutional rights. Eventually, the Supreme Court agreed to hear the case.

Kelo's argument was this: The Fifth Amendment says the government can take private property for "public use," but this land was not being taken for that purpose—it was being taken to build what amounted to a privately owned commercial real estate development in the hope of increasing tax revenues and spurring economic growth. The Founding Fathers had drawn a line, and New London had stepped over it.

"Public Use" Becomes "Public Purpose"

In 2005, by a very contentious 5–4 margin, the Supreme Court ruled against Kelo and in favor of New London. The Supreme Court decided that the meaning of the phrase "public use" in the Constitution also included projects pursued for a "public purpose." Granted, the Court said, the New London project would not be used by the public, like a highway or water plant, but the Fort Trumbull lots were being taken to benefit the public as part of a carefully considered comprehensive economic rejuvenation plan that would serve the public's need for new jobs and increased tax revenue. For five of the nine justices, that "public purpose" was enough of a "public use" to satisfy the Fifth Amendment.

Justice O'Connor wrote a vigorous dissenting opinion. "The specter of condemnation hangs over all property," she wrote. "Nothing is to prevent the state from replacing any Motel 6 with a Ritz-Carlton, any home with a shopping mall, or any farm with a factory." She was particularly troubled by the potential for what the decision would mean to citizens who did not wield power among public officials. "The beneficiaries are likely to be those citizens with disproportionate influence and power in the political process, including large corporations and development firms," O'Connor wrote. "As for the victims, the government now has license to transfer property from those with fewer resources to those with more. The founders cannot have intended this perverse result."

Justice Thomas stated his dissenting view with equal force: "Something has gone seriously awry with this Court's interpretation of the Constitution. Though citizens are safe from the government in their homes, the homes themselves are not."

The *Kelo* decision has been welcomed by state and local officials who have been struggling with economic redevelopment projects. At the same time, anti-*Kelo* forces are hard at work: according to a 2007 report by the Castle Coalition, over forty states have passed some form of anti-*Kelo* legislation, with varying degrees of efficacy.

In the meantime, there is good news and bad news. The good news is that, depending on where you live, it may be easier for federal, state, and local governments to pursue economic revitalization projects. The bad news is that, as part of the process, your backyard may end up in the middle of a factory or hotel lobby.

So, did the Fort Trumbull project that birthed the *Kelo* decision benefit New London? As reported by the Yale Law Journal in July 2015, "The project site is now a field of weeds, a home for feral cats, and, occasionally, a dumping ground for storm debris. The original developer disappeared long ago, as have a string of subsequent developers, none of who have been able to finance the project. The only construction on the site has been some renovation of a building that New London obtained from the federal government. There has been no development at all on any property acquired by eminent domain or under threat of eminent domain."

23. You Can Sue City Hall

Monroe v. Pape (1961)

What happens when the government, which is responsible for creating the law, then violates the law? The Supreme Court sets limits on how far government can intrude into your life, but what are your rights if the government oversteps its boundaries?

As a practical matter, your right to hold the government accountable for its actions was uncertain and unpredictable, until the case of *Monroe v. Pape.* The *Monroe* case applies in a variety of contexts ranging from unlawful restrictions on businesses and property owners, to violations of the rights of criminal defendants. In any discussion concerning the boundaries of the government's power over businesses and individuals under the Due Process Clause, the Commerce Clause, or any other portion of the Constitution, *Monroe* answers the key question: what can those whose rights have been violated do about it?

In the *Monroe* case, thirteen Chicago police officers broke into the Monroe family's home in the early morning without a warrant, routed the occupants from bed, made them stand naked in the living room, and ransacked every room, emptying drawers and ripping mattress covers. Mr. Monroe was then taken to the police station, detained for ten hours while he was interrogated about a two-day-old murder without being permitted to call his family or attorney, and then released without criminal charges being brought against him.

Monroe sued the police officers for damages in federal court, under a post–Civil War statute generally referred to today as "Section 1983." Monroe chose this strategy, as opposed to filing a lawsuit in the local state court, because under state law his chances of successfully suing state officials or employees were slim, and he believed that local state court judges might be prone to protect local police officers.

Section 1983, originally called "the Ku Klux Klan Act of 1871," was enacted by Congress to address the fact that many Southern states were refusing to protect freed blacks from whippings, lynchings, and other atrocities at the hands of whites, mainly Klan members. Monroe took the position that Section 1983 was more than an anachronism limited to the unusual circumstances of the post–Civil War era, and that it gave all persons whose constitutional rights were violated a federal right to sue for damages in federal court.

Using the Power of the Government Against the Government

Monroe v. Pape eventually reached the Supreme Court, and, in a 1961 landmark ruling, Monroe won. The Supreme Court ruled that Section 1983 allowed individuals to bring federal court lawsuits for damages as the result of any "misuse of power" by state officials "clothed with the authority of state law." In 1971, the Supreme Court extended this ruling to allow claims in federal courts against not only state officials, but federal officials as well, in the case of *Bivens v. Six Unknown Named Agents of Federal Bureau of Narcotics.*

In the wake of *Monroe* and *Bivens*, literally thousands of Section 1983 cases have been successfully filed against government officials in federal courts for claimed violations of constitutional rights, such as actions based on unlawful searches, unlawful arrests, police brutality, arbitrary regulation of business and property, improper taxation, governmental dishonesty, and much more.

At their core, the *Monroe* and *Bivens* decisions allow individuals whose constitutional rights have been violated to use the power of the government against the government—a remarkable characteristic of our democracy that we have come to take for granted. This, in turn, has had a predictable effect on government accountability: faced with the prospect of having to explain their actions to a federal court jury, government officials become much more cautious before trifling with individual rights. For this reason, many commentators view *Monroe* and *Bivens* as being among the most significant decisions of the century.

VETO.

CONSTITUTION
of the
UNITED STATES
of America.

Virtue Liberty and Independence

Internal Improvements

U.S. Bank

CHAPTER 8

LIMITING THE IMPERIAL PRESIDENCY

"When the President does it,
that means that it is not illegal."

—RICHARD M. NIXON, U.S. PRESIDENT, 1969–74

Those who've occupied the White House have often tried to expand the scope of their authority. Many have taken the position that the president is wholly independent and has the right to do what he thinks best, without having to answer to the other branches of government.

When the framers of the Constitution, steeped in English law, gathered in Philadelphia to debate and draft the Constitution, they were familiar with such governmental philosophies. For centuries, English law provided that "the king can do no wrong," and untold generations suffered the consequences of an unchecked monarchy. The English emasculated that principle when they enacted the Magna Carta in 1215, creating many of the fundamental rights that eventually found their way into our Constitution. To be sure, the framers had their disagreements over how powerful the president should be, but no one held out for the creation of an infallible monarchy—much, very much, the opposite.

The fact that the president can do wrong, however, raises difficult questions about our system of checks and balances. Who decides if the president is wrong? How do you keep politics out of the process? What if national security is at stake? Not surprisingly, it has been, and will continue to be, the Supreme Court that answers these questions.

A ca. 1833 caricature of President Andrew Jackson as a despotic monarch, probably issued during the fall of 1833 in response to the president's September order to remove federal deposits from the Bank of the United States.

24. The Steel-Seizure Case: How Far Can the President Go in the Name of National Security?

Youngstown Sheet & Tube Co. v. Sawyer (1952)

In June 1950, North Korea invaded South Korea, and the Korean War was on. As the conflict raged, the collective bargaining agreement between the United Steel Workers and the steel industry was due to expire, and the union demanded a substantial raise, which the steel industry refused. Attempts at settlement failed, and on April 4, 1952, the union gave notice of a nationwide steel strike to commence on April 9, 1952.

Steel was an indispensable component of the war effort, and President Truman believed that a work stoppage would jeopardize national security. Citing his authority under "the Constitution and laws of the United States, and as President of the United States and Commander in Chief of the Armed Forces," just a few hours before the strike was to begin Truman issued an executive order directing Secretary of Commerce Charles Sawyer to seize the steel mills from their owners. Truman explained his actions to the American people in a radio and television address, speaking of the grave dangers that would face the nation if the steel companies ceased production.

Less than an hour after Truman concluded his broadcast, attorneys for the steel companies appeared at the home of a federal trial court judge in Washington, D.C., and requested an injunction prohibiting Truman's actions. They rightly pointed out that Congress had never passed a law authorizing a president to unilaterally seize control of an industry, no matter the circumstances, and they asked that their property be returned to them immediately. What, they asked, were the limits of the president's power?

The conflict gave rise to the case of *Youngstown Sheet & Tube Co. v. Sawyer*, better known as the Steel Seizure Case. In the midst of blaring headlines and a rancorous national debate, it was once again left to the judiciary to write the rule book by which Congress and the president would be authorized to govern the country. The issues in the Steel Seizure Case were of such importance that the Supreme Court heard and decided the case just two months after the steel companies' lawyers appeared at the trial court judge's Washington home.

When the case got to the Supreme Court, Truman, through government lawyers, argued for the supremacy of the executive branch: In times of national emergency, the president has the power, and even the obligation, to step in and take action, and neither the Congress nor the judiciary has the constitutional right to stop him. Truman's argument did not depend on legal niceties. When there is a true crisis, he contended, a president must have the right to do what he thinks is right, without having to seek and wait for approval from the other branches of government.

The Supreme Court disagreed. After hearing two days of oral argument, it ruled against Truman by a 6–3 vote.

The "Zone of Twilight"

Justice Black wrote the majority opinion. He began with the foundational proposition that a president is not all-powerful, no matter the circumstances. A president cannot take action, said Justice Black, unless that action is authorized either by a statute passed by Congress, or the Constitution. Plainly, there was no statute authorizing a president to unilaterally seize private property (let alone an entire industry); whatever statutory authority there was *protected* private property from governmental seizure. The question, then, was whether the Constitution itself empowered Truman to seize the steel mills.

Truman's lawyers focused on Article II of the Constitution, which appoints the president as the commander in chief. They contended that the commander in chief must have broad, expansive powers, as would a general on a battlefield. Justice Black, in terse language, rejected this argument and ruled that the power of a commander in chief cannot extend so far as to allow the taking of private property in the name of national security. "This," he said, "is a job for the Nation's lawmakers, not its military authorities."

Justice Jackson, while concurring in the overall result, wrote a separate opinion which, over the years, has become much more influential than Justice Black's reasoning. Justice Jackson wrote that a president's powers are at their maximum when he seeks to enforce plainly expressed congressional will, and those powers are at their "lowest ebb" when he seeks to act against the will of Congress. But, he said, "there is a zone of twilight" between these extremes, and the limits of presidential power in these gray areas "is likely to depend on the imperatives of events"—that is, the president has some room to move in cases of true national emergency, so long as he does not directly violate the plainly expressed will of the Congress.

Justice Jackson concluded that Congress had in prior laws forbidden unilateral seizures of property, and for that reason Truman's actions had to be overturned. But the implication was that if Congress had not plainly expressed its will on this very issue—that is, if Truman had been operating in the "zone of twilight"—Truman might well have been free to do as he thought best in view of the national security issues he faced. The message to both future members of Congress and future presidents was unmistakable.

Truman immediately complied with the Supreme Court's ruling. A fifty-three-day steel strike ensued, no steel shortage occurred, and a settlement was ultimately reached.

National Security Versus Civil Rights:
The Beat Goes On

How far a president can go in the name of national security, and the extent to which Congress can rein in executive powers during such times, has always been and will remain a vital national issue of daunting complexity. There is, of course, no singular formula that can define the proper spheres of executive and congressional authority in all circumstances—particularly when, as is so often the case, the dispute resides in the "zone of twilight" described by Justice Jackson.

As recently as 2004, however, the Supreme Court again stressed that the president's powers are limited by law, even in wartime. Justice O'Connor, referencing the Steel Seizure Case, made quick work of President Bush's contention that he could hold suspected terrorists without a hearing. "We have long since made clear that a state of war is not a blank check for the president when it comes to the rights of the Nation's citizens."

In 2005 and 2006, the Steel Seizure Case again took center stage during the confirmation hearings for Justice Alito and the Senate hearings on the Bush administration's domestic surveillance programs. Senator Arlen Specter stated at the commencement of the Alito hearing: "This hearing comes at a time of great national concern about the balance between civil rights and the president's national security authority." He went on to say, "The president's constitutional war powers as commander in chief to conduct electronic surveillance appear to conflict with congressional legislation in the Foreign Intelligence Surveillance Act. This conflict could activate the considerations raised in Justice Jackson's historic concurrence in the Youngstown Steel Seizure Case. . . . It is a critical analysis for, as Justice Jackson noted: 'What is at stake is the equilibrium established by our constitutional system.'"

The Steel Seizure Case continues to give Congress and the judiciary ample ammunition with which to challenge an exercise of presidential power that arguably oversteps legal boundaries. For example, in 2014, in *NLRB v. Noel Canning*, the Supreme Court unanimously rebuked President Obama's use of so-called recess appointments to fill positions that would normally require the Senate's consent, and in 2016—through a 4–4 vote (taken while the Senate refused to consider President Obama's appointment of a replacement for Justice Scalia) that left a lower court ruling in place—the Supreme Court effectively invalidated President Obama's immigration plan. How such confrontations are resolved in the future will depend on an array of variables, such as whether the challenged presidential action impinges on individual civil liberties, whether it affects only foreign affairs or also domestic affairs, the immediacy and risks of the crisis at hand, and, of course, the personal predilections, backgrounds, and philosophies of the justices who make up the Supreme Court at any given time.

25. Nixon, Executive Privilege, and the Watergate Scandal

United States v. Nixon (1974)

Can the president withhold information from Congress merely because he is the president? Can the president override congressional efforts to oversee the legality of what he does? The inglorious Watergate scandal ultimately forced the Supreme Court to confront these issues in the most dramatic constitutional crisis since the Civil War.

A "Third-Rate Burglary"

In June 1972, during the Nixon–McGovern presidential campaign, five men with cameras and listening devices were arrested inside the Democratic National Committee's offices, located in the Watergate complex in Washington. Thanks in large part to dogged investigative reporting by the *Washington Post* (as portrayed in the book and movie *All the President's Men*), the burglars were publicly linked to Nixon's reelection committee and administration officials. Despite the administration's denials of any involvement (Nixon's press secretary dismissed the break-in as "a third-rate burglary"), public pressure mounted, and a Senate committee conducted an investigation, followed by hearings in 1973.

The hearings were televised, and they captivated the nation. As millions of citizens watched, various Nixon administration officials, including John Dean, Nixon's former counsel, claimed that Nixon's closest associates—and perhaps Nixon himself—had orchestrated a cover-up of the break-in and engaged in a host of other illegal activities. Nixon was clearly in the Senate's sights: Senator Howard Baker repeatedly asked witnesses the question that has since worked its way into the nation's political lexicon: "What did the president know, and when did he know it?"

During an otherwise routine July 1973 hearing session, one of Nixon's assistants, Alexander Butterfield, revealed that Nixon had installed a taping system in the Oval Office and had retained possession of the very tapes that would definitively and undeniably answer Senator Baker's famous question. Butterfield's revelation changed the nature of the Senate inquiry—why ask witnesses what Nixon had been told and what he had said in the Oval Office, when there existed the ultimate original source material, a tape recording?

The "Saturday Night Massacre"

By this time, honoring a promise he had made during his Senate confirmation hearings, Attorney General Elliot Richardson had appointed Archibald Cox, a well-known lawyer, to serve as a special prosecutor investigating the Watergate case. Shortly after Butterfield's testimony, Cox served a subpoena on the White House, demanding the tapes. The battle was under way.

Nixon refused to produce the tapes, citing a murky legal doctrine known as "executive privilege." He contended that each branch of government was separate from the other and legally entitled to be free from interference by the other. In fact, Nixon knew that, among many other embarrassments, the tapes included the "smoking gun," conversations in which Nixon sought to use the CIA to unlawfully obstruct the FBI's investigation of the Watergate burglary in the effort to hide the involvement of his administration and, perhaps, himself.

Nixon offered Cox a compromise involving a screening of the tapes by a Nixon senatorial ally and the production of edited versions. Cox refused.

The next night, October 23, 1973, a Saturday, Nixon ordered Attorney General Richardson to fire Cox. In view of the promise he had made to Congress, Richardson refused and, in protest, resigned. Nixon then ordered Deputy Attorney General William Ruckelshaus to fire Cox. Ruckelshaus refused, and resigned as well. Nixon then ordered the Solicitor General, Robert Bork, to fire Cox. Bork was, by default, now in charge of the Justice Department and he, too, considered resigning. Bork, unlike Richardson, would not be violating a commitment to the Senate if he obeyed the order, and Richardson persuaded him to comply, for fear that the Justice Department would otherwise be thrown into turmoil. Bork reluctantly fired Cox, culminating what has been dubbed the "Saturday Night Massacre."

Congress was outraged, and various bills of impeachment were eventually introduced, charging the president with, among other things, abuses of power and obstruction of justice. The battle had escalated into a full-fledged war between Congress and the president.

The firing of Cox did Nixon no good and a lot of harm. Cox's successor, Leon Jaworski, doggedly pushed for the production of the tapes, and public pressure crescendoed. Nixon backpedaled, releasing edited transcripts of the tapes. The transcripts corroborated much of what Dean and many witnesses had stated, and also included a very suspicious eighteen-minute gap, which Nixon blamed on his secretary, further fanning public cynicism and outrage.

Jaworski sought a court order compelling Nixon to obey the subpoena. Now all three branches of government were involved in the conflagration. Nixon again relied on "executive privilege," arguing that neither he nor any other president could fulfill the duties of the office if private conversations and planning sessions were subject to public disclosure. Nixon contended that he led a separate branch of government, and that the other branches, Congress and the courts, had no right to compel him to take actions he felt to be unwarranted.

The lower courts entered orders, appeals were filed, and a major constitutional crisis loomed. It ultimately fell to the Supreme Court to define the boundaries of congressional, presidential, and judicial power.

The Supreme Court's Decision: A President, Not a Monarch

It is now known that as they debated the case, the justices had substantial disagreements among themselves, but agreed that they had to speak with one voice. Nixon had publicly agreed to accept a "definitive" order from the Court, and the justices feared that if their opinion were not unanimous, Nixon would use that as a basis on which to defy the Court's order. This raised the specter of Congress and the Court sending federal marshals to remove the tapes from the White House, and the president, as commander in chief, mustering armed forces to guard the Oval Office. It was a risk the Court knew it could not take, and the justices managed to set aside their differences and reach a unanimous and clear result.

Chief Justice Warren Burger announced the Court's decision on July 24, 1974: Nixon was ordered to surrender the tapes.

The Court recognized that a president could insist on a right to confidentiality in some circumstances, such as to protect national security—a concept later presidents have attempted to use when called upon to disclose their personal documents and records. Nixon, however, had not sought to avoid the subpoena on these grounds but, rather, claimed that executive privilege was absolute, that as the leader of an independent branch of government he could withhold what he wanted. Nixon's lawyer explained Nixon's position in his argument before the Supreme Court: "The President wants me to argue that he is as powerful a monarch as Louis XIV, only four years at a time, and is not subject to the processes of any court in the land except the court of impeachment."

The Supreme Court disagreed, ruling that a president is not above the law, and, when faced with a subpoena issued to obtain evidence in an investigation of national importance with criminal implications, he must comply, as must any other citizen.

To his credit, Nixon complied less than a week later. The House Judiciary Committee had already begun impeachment proceedings, and Nixon knew that the evidence on the tapes would seal his fate. On August 8, 1974, reading the writing on the wall, Nixon resigned— the first president ever to do so. Vice President Gerald Ford assumed the presidency.

After being sworn in by Chief Justice Burger, President Ford announced that "our long national nightmare is over." As much as anything else, the "nightmare" was the prospect that the branches of government would defy each other, and that their disagreements could, literally, result in a confrontation of force. That did not happen, leading President Ford to emotionally, and correctly, observe, "Our Constitution works; our great Republic is a government of laws and not of men."

On September 8, 1974, Ford pardoned Nixon for any crimes he might have committed in the Watergate affair.

26. Who Writes the Rules of War?

Boumediene v. Bush (2008)
Al Odah v. U.S. (2008)

In retrospect, it seems right that President Truman should not have had the unilateral authority to nationalize an entire industry by edict, and that President Nixon should not have had the right to cloak the presidency with the prerogatives of eighteenth-century monarchs. Our traditions respect strong leadership but disdain power grabs. In situations like these, there is something in our American DNA that calls out for the Supreme Court to intervene and recalibrate the delicate balance between the powers of presidents and the rule of law.

But what about the conduct of wars? The Constitution establishes the president as the commander in chief and provides Congress with wartime funding and oversight responsibilities. Does the Supreme Court have the right to look over their shoulders and review how the president and Congress choose to fight?

A New Kind of War

Shortly after the 9/11 attacks, the Bush administration began a global effort to round up suspected terrorists. It cast a wide net—such is the difficulty of fighting dispersed armies of nonuniformed twenty-first-century terrorists—and many people who had done little more than occupy the wrong place at the wrong time were ensnared.

According to international law, "enemy combatants" can be held as prisoners of war. But under the Geneva Convention, those who claim not to be enemy combatants are to be given a full hearing, including basic rights of due process, so they have an opportunity to prove their innocence.

Many of the suspects rounded up after 9/11 claimed that they were not enemy combatants, and yet they were imprisoned without any hearing. The Bush administration offered an explanation based on practicalities. Unlike conventional warfare, where uniformed enemy combatants can be captured on the battlefield, terrorists fade into the background, often far from the scenes of their crimes, and it can be impossible to tell the terrorists from the bystanders. The full-scale hearings contemplated by the Geneva Convention could no longer be justified and would compromise fundamental antiterrorism strategies. Thousands of lives were at risk: the terrorists were fighting a new kind of war; the old rules of law no longer applied.

The Bush administration suspected that it might be on thin legal ice, and its lawyers struggled to find a way to further justify its position. They did not have much to go on; but, ultimately, they crafted (some would say manufactured) a legal rationale. Initially, they contended that the Geneva Convention only applies to combatants who fight for nations that have signed it, and not to terrorists who are affiliated with no government and can surface from virtually anywhere. But recognizing that U.S. courts might not agree, they also argued that noncitizen foreign detainees do not have the right to challenge their status and treatment in our judicial system—and even if they did, they most certainly had no such right if they were held overseas, not on American soil. In effect, the position espoused by the Bush administration lawyers was, "we might be wrong, but there's nothing the detainees can do about it."

Based on these legal positions, the Bush administration constructed a terrorist detention facility at the U.S. naval base at Guantánamo Bay, Cuba; continued to hold the detainees without hearings; and steadfastly claimed that whatever went on there was outside the reach of American law . . . whatever happens in Guantánamo, stays in Guantánamo. One administration official told the press that Guantánamo was the legal equivalent of "outer space."

The Governmental Face-Off Begins

The expected legal challenges were filed shortly after the first detainees arrived at Guantánamo in early 2002. By 2004, the first wave of these cases had made their way to the Supreme Court which, in the case of *Rasul v. Bush*, dealt the Bush administration a stinging setback: The Court ruled that American officials could not lock up foreign detainees, whether in the United States or in Guantánamo, without some demonstrated reason, and that the foreign detainees had a right to a reasonable military commission hearing so they could challenge the accusations being made against them. U.S. officials acting in the name of the U.S. government must comply with U.S. law, no matter where they conduct their business.

The Bush administration (along with much of Congress) acted immediately to parry the Supreme Court's thrust. It initiated military-run "combatant status review tribunals" (CSRTs), to ostensibly provide the detainees with a military commission hearing that satisfied legal standards. In fact, however, the CSRTs ran hearings in name only— they were one-sided proceedings, held in secrecy, in which the detainees were given virtually no rights to review and confront whatever evidence the military chose to present against them.

In 2006, the Supreme Court agreed to review a challenge to the CSRTs in the case of *Hamdan v. Rumsfeld*. Hamdan was a Yemeni national who admitted that he had at one time been Osama bin Laden's driver but who denied any terrorist activities.

In *Hamdan*, a bare majority of the Supreme Court saw the situation as another *Youngstown Sheet & Tube* case. The Uniform Code of Military Justice, enacted by Congress long before, required military commissions such as the CSRTs to comply with the Geneva Convention, which mandated hearings that included a meaningful right to challenge and present evidence. Faced with what it saw as a plain expression of congressional will, the majority reined in President Bush just as it had reined in President Truman: The executive branch is not free to disregard Congress except in the face of truly exigent circumstances, the Court said, and there was no proof that national security would be compromised if Guantánamo detainees were afforded a fair hearing at which they had a genuine opportunity to prove that they were not terrorists.

The dissenters disagreed, calling the majority's view "patently erroneous." They argued that such matters were outside the Supreme Court's sphere of influence, and stressed that the *Youngstown Sheet & Tube* decision, properly interpreted, required "a heavy measure of deference" to the president, the commander in chief, in time of real war. This was serious business in which judges have no place, they stressed, and the Supreme Court needed to stay out of it.

The ball was back in the Bush administration's court, and at the president's urging Congress quickly passed another law, the Military Commissions Act. It added a bit more due process to the proceedings, but essentially left the Bush administration's system intact. Now the legal fundamentals had shifted: No longer could the president be charged with disregarding the will of Congress; instead, the president and the Congress were on precisely the same page.

In response, a new lawsuit was filed, involving thirty-seven Guantánamo detainees. The case was brought in the name of two of them: Lakhdar Boumediene, an Algerian taken from Bosnia in October 2001; and Fawzi Khalid Abdullah Fahad Al Odah, a Kuwaiti captured in Afghanistan in 2001. Both claimed they were innocent, and they each sought a hearing so they could prove it.

The *Boumediene* and *Al Odah* cases crystallized a different issue, involving the fundamentals of our tripartite form of government. In *Hamdan*, the Supreme Court had served as a sort of governmental referee—it found that the executive branch had gone rogue and improperly overstepped the directives of the legislative branch. But now the executive and legislative branches had joined forces. In times of war, shouldn't that be good enough? Does the Supreme Court have the right to tell the other branches how to fight a war?

The rule of law applies in both war and peace, said the lawyers representing the detainees. The fact that the president and the Congress now agree does not end the inquiry. The *real* question is this: Does their agreement violate the Constitution? The Supreme Court has both the power and the obligation to answer that question, they argued. It cannot sit on the sidelines.

Still, as the dissenters had argued in *Hamdan*, was this, the conduct of war, really any of the Supreme Court's business? Doesn't there come a point when national security trumps constitutional niceties?

The "Great Writ"

The *Boumediene* and *Al Odah* cases focused squarely on the bedrock constitutional right of "habeas corpus." Habeas corpus (Latin for "you have the body") has deep roots in fundamental Anglo-American traditions. Rightly known as the "Great Writ," it was originally conceived as a means to keep the Crown from arbitrarily imprisoning its enemies without due process. Today, it remains a bodyguard of key personal freedoms—anyone being held in custody can file a habeas corpus petition and have an independent judge review the legality of his detention. If, for instance, a police officer or district attorney locks you up because of a personal vendetta, or because of your race or religion, or to quell political opposition, or based on phony evidence, habeas corpus is your last (and often best) line of defense. It is designed to be the constitutional antidote to injustices involving personal liberty, and the Constitution itself mandates that it may be suspended only in the case of "rebellion or invasion."

If the right of habeas corpus provides anything, the *Boumediene* and *Al Odah* lawyers argued, it provides people like the detainees in Guantánamo with the right to challenge the government's decision to imprison them without a proven reason to do so. Yes, we're involved in a war on terrorism, but fundamental rights remain fundamental rights, no matter the unpopularity of those who seek to assert them. Indeed, the right of habeas corpus was designed to protect the very people the government would prefer to leave unprotected.

But, still, an overriding issue remained: Do foreigners—noncitizens who have never set foot on American soil, who were captured as part of the government's efforts to prevent another terrorist attack, and who are being held offshore by the military during wartime—have the right of habeas corpus?

On the one hand, the president and Congress have the constitutional responsibility to defend the nation, and the military has the acknowledged expertise. Can habeas corpus be used to subject their decisions to review by judges who sit safely behind a mahogany bench?

But on the other hand, there is the Constitution. Are the risks to national security even greater if we allow the very persons and institutions sworn to defend the Constitution to erode the rights it provides?

The Ruling: A Constitution without Boundaries

In a 5–4 decision replete with strident, sometimes apocalyptic dissents, the Supreme Court ruled that the Constitution's reach was limited by neither geography nor war, and it does not allow the government to imprison *anyone*, citizen or noncitizen, in war or peace, domestically or abroad, without the basic due process civilized societies recognize as being elemental to any meaningful effort to find the truth. The Court ruled that the one-sided hearings implemented by the Bush administration were fundamentally unfair and, in the absence of lawful military commission hearings, the Guantánamo detainees (and, by plain implication, detainees being held as suspected terrorists anywhere else in the world) *did* have a habeas corpus right under the Constitution to challenge their detention in United States civilian courts.

Justice Anthony Kennedy, writing for the majority, summarized his view of the inevitable conflicts between national security and individual liberties that brought the Guantánamo detainees before the nation's highest court: "The laws and Constitution are designed to survive, and remain in force, in extraordinary times." The branches of government, he warned, may not "switch the Constitution on or off at will."

Chief Justice Roberts attacked the majority for not allowing the bipartisan legislation crafted by the executive and legislative branches to be fully implemented and vetted by lower courts before being dismantled by the Supreme Court. He charged that the majority was more concerned about flexing its judicial muscles than protecting the detainees. The ruling, he concluded, "is not really about the detainees at all, but about control of federal policy regarding enemy combatants." He expressed concern that the public will "lose a bit more control over the conduct of this nation's foreign policy to unelected, politically unaccountable judges."

Justice Scalia was less diplomatic. He excoriated the majority's ruling—the unique nature of terrorism requires military, not judicial, solutions, he reasoned—and he predicted that "devastating" and "disastrous consequences" would flow from the decision. "It will almost certainly cause more Americans to be killed."

Justice Kennedy was not moved. Obviously influenced by the fact that many of the detainees had been imprisoned for six years without any meaningful hearing, he concluded that the Supreme Court had to act without further delay. "Within the Constitution's separation-of-powers structure, few exercises of judicial power are as legitimate or as necessary as the responsibility to hear challenges to the authority of the Executive to imprison a person."

Will Terrorists Go Free?

Contrary to some reports, the decision does not mean that the Guantánamo detainees must be released; it means only that they (and other detainees, no matter where held) are entitled to a hearing, including the basic rights and safeguards Americans take for granted, for the purpose of determining whether they are enemy combatants or innocent bystanders. The alternative is the endorsement of a policy in which suspected combatants are held indefinitely, like prisoners in a dungeon, until we unilaterally determine what to do with them.

But what about the practicalities and the real, palpable national security concerns? The government will bear the burden of proving that there is a basis to continue to hold each of the detainees; if it cannot do so, then they *will* be freed. Will our government be forced to disclose classified information and intelligence-gathering techniques in order to prove its case? Proving that a farmer is also a terrorist can be difficult: Where will the evidence come from? Will our most covert and specialized military and intelligence personnel be forced to testify and undergo cross-examination about what they know and how they know it? What if a terrorist confessed to an American interrogator, but without having been given a Miranda warning? Suppose a detainee, while not a terrorist himself, has crucial information: Will that be a basis on which continued detention is permitted? Will information obtained through so-called "coercive" interrogation methods be admissible? If there's solid evidence that an individual is a terrorist, but we can't fully prove it, will the individual be set free, no matter the security risks?

Since the *Boumediene* and *Al Odah* decisions, the vast majority of detainees have lost their habeas corpus cases. In 2012, the Supreme Court refused to accept the appeal of seven Guantánamo detainees and allowed a series of rulings by lower courts to stand, making it increasingly difficult for detainees to win their cases. At that time, the *Christian Science Monitor* reported that between 2008 and July 2010, Guantánamo detainees won 56 percent of their habeas corpus challenges, but after July 2010, the win rate fell to 8 percent—a federal judge sided with only one of twelve detainees.

So What? How Does This Affect Your Life?

Why would two cases dealing with the rights of suspected terrorists being held in Cuba be included in a book that focuses on the Supreme Court cases that most directly affect your life?

Consider this question on two levels.

First, in the coming years, few things may affect the lives of Americans more than the success or failure of our efforts to defeat international terrorism. A keystone of those efforts has been measures designed to win the so-called "hearts and minds" of the populations in which terrorism flourishes by convincing them that democracies in general, and America in particular, respect individual freedoms and promote justice. The message is that there is a better way, our way. But many analysts believe that institutions like Guantánamo have inexorably eroded our credibility by displaying to the world that in reality we do not practice what we preach: rather than standing for fundamental liberties and human rights, Guantánamo has allowed our adversaries to convincingly portray us as a society that incarcerates individuals on the basis of mere suspicion without a meaningful effort to determine if that incarceration is warranted.

Will the fact that we will now afford the detainees full and honest due process hearings, and that we will close Guantánamo, change that perception and elevate our standing among those we seek to influence? Will whatever salutary effects the decision produces be counterbalanced by the release of dangerous terrorists, or by the extent to which it may hamstring the military's effort to obtain crucial intelligence and take terrorists out of circulation? There is, of course, no way to know, and much will depend on the related policies adopted by future administrations.

But both the Supreme Court majority and the minority agree on this: the decision represents a searing rebuke of the way both the executive and the Congress have conducted themselves since 9/11, and it will have a major effect on how the government conducts itself in the future, for better (if you believe the majority) or worse (if you believe the minority).

Second, whether justified (as the majority contends) or unjustified (as the minority contends), the decision represents an extremely significant assertion of Supreme Court authority in respect to the president and the Congress—some commentators, perhaps a bit overwrought, have called it the most significant redefinition of the balance of power in at least a half century. Will the Supreme Court's refusal to yield to presidential or congressional judgments on national security continue? Will rulings on the constitutionality of "coercive interrogation techniques" and other tactics used in the war on terror be next? Will an emboldened Supreme Court expand its reach into other areas of international policy? Or are the *Boumediene* and *Al Odah* decisions an aberration that will be limited to the unusual and extreme plight of some of the Guantánamo detainees?

CHAPTER 9

HOW FREE IS FREE SPEECH?

*"If liberty means anything at all, it means the right
to tell people what they do not want to hear."*

—GEORGE ORWELL, BRITISH AUTHOR AND JOURNALIST

The First Amendment prohibits the government from "abridging the freedom of speech." It is difficult to overstate the importance of this precept to the Founding Fathers and to our survival as a democracy.

But as the aphorism about yelling "Fire!" in a crowded theater makes evident, free speech cannot always be so free. Speech, for instance, can take the form of calls to violence and anarchy, endangering entire communities. Speech can be obscene past the point of imagining and repugnant to the values that hold a society intact. Speech can endanger children.

Underregulation of speech can be dangerous. Overregulation of speech can be more dangerous. It is the Supreme Court's unenviable job to determine where you draw the line.

A group of diverse Americans raises the Old Glory in this poster commemorating the Fourth of July, 1876; is burning this flag an act of free speech?

27. The Right to Be Repugnant

Brandenburg v. Ohio (1969)

In the 1960s, Clarence Brandenburg was a well-known leader of an Ohio Ku Klux Klan group. He invited a reporter to film various Klan activities, such as a cross-burning attended by armed men. In the film, Brandenburg, in Klan regalia, made a speech threatening vengeance if the president, Congress, and Supreme Court "continues to suppress the white, Caucasian race." Brandenburg also advocated that blacks be transported to Africa and Jews be sent to Israel.

In the early 1900s, Ohio, like nineteen other states, enacted what was then known as a "criminal syndicalism" statute. Ohio's statute made it a crime to advocate "the duty, necessity, or propriety of crime, sabotage, violence, or unlawful methods of terrorism as a means of accomplishing industrial or political reform," and to assemble with a group for such purposes. After the film became public, Brandenburg was arrested and convicted under the Ohio statute, and sentenced to a fine and imprisonment.

Brandenburg challenged the constitutionality of the Ohio statute, claiming that it infringed on his basic First Amendment right to free speech. The Ohio courts turned down Brandenburg's appeal, and the Supreme Court then agreed to hear the case.

Only in America: The Right to Advocate Revolution

In its 1969 decision in *Brandenburg v. Ohio*, the Supreme Court unanimously invalidated Brandenburg's conviction. The Court ruled that "mere advocacy" is free speech protected by the First Amendment and it cannot be punished—even when the speaker is advocating the use of force or the violation of law. Only advocacy that is "directed to inciting or producing imminent lawless action and is likely to incite or produce such action" can be restricted—what courts often call "fighting words." This is a crucial, constitutional line in the sand, and the Court ruled that any law or act of a government official that fails to appreciate this distinction "sweeps within its condemnation speech which our Constitution has immunized from governmental control."

Brandenburg exemplifies how far the Supreme Court will go to insulate speech from government interference, a perspective that carries over into many other arenas, such as the Court's reluctance to delve as deeply into the regulation of obscenity as many people feel it should. The decision stands as the Supreme Court's last word on the broad protections the First Amendment provides to speech that advocates force or lawlessness to effectuate social change.

Fundamentally, *Brandenburg* provides a constitutional safe haven for virtually all speech that communicates an idea or position, no matter how repugnant. Our traditions so respect the right of free speech that our government will protect even those who espouse that it be overthrown.

28. Obscenity and the First Amendment

Miller v. California (1973)

One of the linchpins of a democratic society is this: people must know, clearly and in advance, what conduct can be prosecuted by the government as a crime, and what conduct is lawful. If the definitions are vague and blurry, the government can arrest whomever they don't like whenever they wish, and citizens must walk on eggshells for fear of recrimination, which is how dictatorships remain in power. Few scenarios could be more violative of the "government of laws, not men" envisioned by the Constitution.

"I Know It When I See It"

Decades ago, the Supreme Court ruled that "obscenity" is not protected by the First Amendment. What that meant as a practical matter was that the federal and state governments could make it a crime to distribute obscene materials, which is exactly what was happening. But how can "obscenity" be defined so that people might know, clearly and in advance, what they could do without risking a jail term? Without a clear definition, the local bookseller would risk a criminal record if he failed to remove from the shelves all of the novels with graphic love scenes (*Madame Bovary? Lolita? Ulysses?*), and the local theater would have to think twice before showing a movie with sexual content (*The Graduate?*). And what about the rights of adults to do what they want in their private lives without the government's "Big Brother" interference?

In a 1964 case, Justice Potter Stewart was asked to decide whether a movie under the Court's review was "hardcore pornography," and he mirrored the maddening difficulty of trying to define what may be indefinable. "I shall not today attempt further to define the kinds of material I understand to be embraced within that shorthand description; and perhaps I could never succeed in intelligibly doing so," he said. "But I know it when I see it, and the motion picture involved in this case is not that."

The "I know it when I see it" test was not exactly the kind of standard that would provide fair notice of the activities that might land you in jail. But Justice Stewart's frustration was understandable: How can words draw clear lines between what is and is not obscene, any more than words can define what is and is not beautiful, or does or does not taste good?

"Movie Day" in the Supreme Court

The upshot of a rule that says you can only know obscenity when you see obscenity is that, eventually, you have to look at obscenity—and through the 1960s that's just what the Supreme Court justices did.

According to various articles and books about the Supreme Court (often based on accounts from former Supreme Court law clerks), many of the justices and their clerks regularly gathered in the Supreme Court basement on what came to be known as "movie days" to review films that were the subject of obscenity prosecutions. Some justices refused to participate. Others took it as a solemn duty. But a few seemed to enjoy their work. Justice Thurgood Marshall, it was said, sat in the front row and joked loudly, even asking for copies of films so he could show his children when they were older. Justice John Marshall Harlan II, who was nearly blind, mischievously sat next to more prudish colleagues and insisted that they narrate the on-screen goings-on, to his great amusement ("Oh, extraordinary!" he would frequently exclaim).

By the early 1970s, the Supreme Court was ready to find a different solution.

Let Someone Else Do It

In 1973, the Supreme Court again tackled the obscenity issue in the case of *Miller v. California*, which continues to represent the last, definitive word on the subject—at least to the extent a 5–4 decision can be "definitive."

Miller was convicted under a California obscenity statute for knowingly selling brochures that displayed men and women engaged in sexual activity. The law at the time stemmed from a 1957 case, *Roth v. United States*. Under *Roth*, in order to be obscene, a court had to find that the "dominant theme taken as a whole appeals to the prurient interest" of the "average person, applying contemporary community standards." Later cases added that only materials that are "patently offensive" and "utterly without redeeming social value" could be obscene.

By 1970, two of the sitting justices, Douglas and Black, believed the First Amendment protected *all* speech, including obscenity, and Justice William Brennan, who had written the *Roth* opinion, had concluded that efforts at definition were fruitless and counterproductive. Chief Justice Burger, however, believed that a framework should be developed that permitted localities to create their own obscenity standards, and he politicked among the justices for a majority vote in favor of that position.

What emerged from an extremely contentious debate among the justices was a bare majority in favor of a three-part test that would define what could be prosecuted as "obscenity":

(a) whether the average person, applying contemporary community standards, would find that the work, taken as a whole, appeals to the prurient interest;

(b) whether the work depicts or describes, in a patently offensive way, sexual conduct specifically defined by the applicable state law;

(c) and whether the work, taken as a whole, lacks serious literary, artistic, political, or scientific value.

If all three criteria were met, the work could be considered obscene, and those who distributed it could be charged with a crime.

In effect, the Supreme Court, while setting some definitional limits, abdicated responsibility for defining obscenity. The upshot of *Miller* was to permit each locality to impose its own definition. What a jury in one locality might consider "prurient" might be considered "literature" in another.

Justice Stewart would no longer be able to know it when he saw it; it would depend on where he was at the time.

Making Obscenity a Federal Case: The New Wave of Prosecutions

The *Miller* decision resulted in literally hundreds of obscenity prosecutions in the few years after the case was decided, until the dust settled and the rules of the game in each community became better known. For many years thereafter, obscenity cases were rare.

That all changed in 2001, when the Bush administration began bringing federal obscenity prosecutions. By way of comparison, there were four obscenity prosecutions during the eight years of the Clinton administration. Between 2001 and mid-2005, the Bush administration obtained more than forty obscenity convictions. Given *Miller*'s focus on community standards, the prosecutions were most often brought in communities believed to be more traditionally conservative, making the prospect of obtaining a conviction more likely. In December 2005, for instance, a Florida man was sentenced to five years in prison by a federal judge in Montana for distributing obscene videotapes throughout the country.

Where all this leaves the obscenity issue may become extremely interesting in the near future. Given the important First Amendment questions that obscenity questions raise, one or more of the Bush administration's obscenity prosecutions could easily find their way to the Supreme Court.

Senators, congressmen, and the media consistently speak of the "conservative" tilt of the Supreme Court in recent years, particularly in view of recent appointments. But the "conservative" label has a different meaning when applied to a Supreme Court justice than it does when used in a political context. A "conservative" politician is often understood as one who favors more "traditional" values, and would seek to prohibit the distribution of sexually explicit materials. A "conservative" jurist, however, is typically regarded as one who takes laws in general, and the Constitution in particular, more literally, without attempting to inject personal values or notions of social justice.

The First Amendment says that the government "shall make no law . . . abridging the freedom of speech." It does not say that the government may make some laws. No law. We may soon see just how "conservative" the Supreme Court really is.

29. The Flag-Burning Case: Can Conduct Be "Free Speech"?

Texas v. Johnson (1969)

The First Amendment protects "freedom of speech," but people often communicate and express themselves in nonverbal ways. For that reason, the Supreme Court has, for many years, recognized that conduct, like gestures or demonstrations, can have a communicative element, and can be "speech" for First Amendment purposes. For instance, the Supreme Court has ruled that when, in the context of a political protest, a student wears a black armband to school in violation of school rules, the student is plainly attempting to communicate an idea, and the armband is "speech" entitled to First Amendment protection.

But how about burning the American flag? Just how far does the First Amendment go?

During the 1984 Republican National Convention in Dallas, Gregory Lee Johnson participated in a demonstration against the Reagan administration and its policies. The demonstration culminated at Dallas City Hall, where Johnson unfurled an American flag, doused it with kerosene, and set it on fire while others chanted "America, the red, white, and blue, we spit on you." No one was injured or threatened, but many were seriously offended.

Johnson was arrested and convicted under a Texas statute, similar to statutes in forty-seven other states, prohibiting the desecration of the flag. He appealed his conviction, and the Supreme Court agreed to hear his case in 1989.

Johnson contended that the Texas statute violated his First Amendment rights of free speech. Johnson argued that what he did was not just an act of meaningless destruction, but was clearly meant to convey a political message protected by the First Amendment.

Texas argued that flag burning cannot be construed as "speech," but even if it were, not all "speech" is protected. The Supreme Court had long ago ruled that speech intended to incite imminent violence or other public harm does not merit First Amendment protection. Texas argued that flag desecration fell within this exception to the First Amendment: the flag represented the nation itself and, consequently, the desecration of the flag was so offensive to so many people that it always involved the threat of violence.

Can Setting a Fire Be "Speech"?

By a bare 5–4 majority, the Supreme Court agreed with Johnson and ruled the Texas statute unconstitutional. Justice Brennan wrote, "If there is a bedrock principle underlying the First Amendment, it is that the Government may not prohibit the expression of an idea simply because society finds the idea itself offensive or disagreeable." He concluded that preserving the fundamental right of freedom of expression, no matter how repugnant that expression may be, was more important than preserving the flag as a symbol of nationhood.

The dissenters were livid. Flag burning is not "speech," Chief Justice Rehnquist wrote, but rather "is the equivalent of an inarticulate grunt or roar" whose only purpose is "not to express any particular idea, but to antagonize others." Johnson was punished not for his ideas, said the dissenters, but for committing an act that is regarded as profoundly repulsive to the majority of citizens—and just as society has the right to legislate against offensive conduct like embezzlement and pollution, it has the right to legislate against flag burning.

The *Texas v. Johnson* decision provoked the House and Senate to pass condemnatory resolutions, and President George H. W. Bush supported a constitutional amendment outlawing flag desecration. Others in Congress supported an anti–flag–burning statute. Those forces prevailed, resulting in the Flag Protection Act of 1989. Almost immediately, that law was challenged, and the Supreme Court ruled it to be unconstitutional on the same bases expressed in the *Texas v. Johnson* decision. Since that time, there have been repeated calls for a constitutional amendment but, to date, proponents have been unable to garner sufficient votes in the House and Senate to force the issue.

As for the line between conduct that is regarded as speech and protected under the First Amendment, and conduct that does not implicate the First Amendment, it is interesting to compare the Supreme Court's 1968 decision in *United States v. O'Brien*. In that case, O'Brien burned his draft card during an anti-war protest, and he was arrested under a federal law making the intentional destruction of a draft card a federal crime. O'Brien's draft-card burning was plainly the same kind of political protest as Johnson's flag burning, but this time the Supreme Court let the conviction stand. The difference, according to the Court, was that Congress had a legitimate interest in the preservation of draft cards in order to assure the efficient operation of the Selective Service System. So, while that element of O'Brien's conduct that was "speech" might be constitutionally protected, there was another element to his conduct that was not "speech" and could be punished.

30. The Freedom to Criticize
Public Officials and Public Figures

New York Times Co. v. Sullivan (1964)

Although the First Amendment protects "free speech," not everything that is said or written is defined as "speech" worthy of a First Amendment shield. Some examples have been discussed previously, like "fighting words" intended to incite immediate violence, or obscenity. Another example stems from the centuries-old common law of defamation: you cannot falsely call someone a thief or an incompetent in public, and then hide behind the First Amendment when you're sued for the damage you did to their reputation. Defamation law covers both false statements made in writing (libel) and false statements made in spoken form (slander). Either way, the law recognizes the right we all have to protect our good names.

At the same time, however, our democracy, like any democracy, depends on the ability of citizens to speak freely about their public officials without fear of reprisal. This is the essence of the First Amendment, and one of the key freedoms that distinguishes us from a dictatorship. But here's the difficult part: What happens if, in the course of speaking out about a public official, you inadvertently say something that turns out to be false? For instance, based on information you got from the town bookkeeper, you honestly think that the tax collector is embezzling tax money, and you say so at a public meeting. The tax collector is fired and his reputation is ruined. It turns out, however, that the bookkeeper was wrong, but you didn't know that at the time.

You certainly had a First Amendment right to speak out, but don't public officials have the right to protect their reputations, like anyone else? And if they do have the right to sue for libel and slander, what effect will that have on the willingness of citizens to freely speak their minds about important issues at the next public meeting?

In 1960, a group seeking, among other things, to raise funds for the legal defense of Martin Luther King Jr. ran a full-page ad in the *New York Times*. The ad included statements that the Montgomery, Alabama, police had engaged in serious acts of misconduct. As it turned out, the statements were false. L. B. Sullivan, the city official who oversaw the police department, brought a libel action against the New York Times, and a local jury awarded him the then-unprecedented sum of $500,000.

Is There a Right to Lie?

The *New York Times* appealed, claiming that the case violated crucial rights of free speech, and the Supreme Court agreed to hear the case. The issue was how the country should balance the First Amendment right to speak out about public officials, against the right of those public officials to protect their reputations from false statements. In its decision, the Supreme Court spoke very clearly about which way that balance should tilt.

Justice Brennan wrote the Court's majority opinion. He began by stating the obvious: "Freedom of expression upon public questions is secured by the First Amendment." But he then went a remarkable step further and ruled that, contrary to the entrenched principles of defamation law, even false statements about public officials would from that time forward be protected by the First Amendment. Justice Brennan wanted to make sure that citizens could speak out about their public officials without having to look over their shoulders. As he put it, even false statements must be protected if this basic right of public discourse is to have the "breathing space" it needs to survive.

But Justice Brennan also set limits: only false statements about public officials *made in good faith* would be protected. No protection would be given to a false statement made with "malice"— that is, with the knowledge that it is false or, very important, with "reckless disregard" of whether it is false.

The *New York Times Co. v. Sullivan* limitation on defamation suits by public officials was extended in later cases to also include "public figures"—movie stars, people frequently in the media, and so on. The logic is that when you are in the public spotlight, the public should have a First Amendment right to talk about you in good faith, without fear of lawsuits.

The Real-World Impact of *New York Times Co. v. Sullivan*

Picture a campaign for governor between Sam Smith and John Jones. Smith hires an investigator. The investigator tells Smith that he has evidence documenting that Jones uses cocaine. Smith immediately starts running attack ads, calling Jones the "Cocaine Candidate." Jones loses the election and his reputation is ruined. It turns out that the investigator's information was false—the drug user was a different John Jones, not the candidate. Jones sues Smith for libel. Smith defends by claiming that he placed the ads in good faith, based on the information provided by a professional investigator, and that, under the First Amendment, candidates in an election campaign are allowed to make mistakes. What more could he do?

Jones, however, wants to know whether Smith showed "reckless disregard" for whether or not the reports were false. As Justice Brennan explained, if Smith recklessly disregarded the truth, Smith could be liable to Jones. Did you make sure the investigator corroborated the sources? Did you personally interview any of the people who made the accusation? "John Jones" is a common name; did you do anything to make sure this was not a case of mistaken identity? Or did you just put on blinders because you wanted the information to be true?

The "reckless disregard" issue is the battleground on which these cases are usually fought. It is tough to prove that someone intentionally lied, and the question usually boils down to whether they cared enough about the truth to seek it out. Remember, in order to be liable for defamation of a public official, it takes more than just a disregard for whether a statement is false—it takes a *reckless* disregard, which is a much higher standard.

New York Times Co. v. Sullivan is there when a national news anchor reports a story on congressional misconduct; or when a local newspaper reporter attempts to expose a municipal conflict of interest; or when a citizen comes to a town meeting to complain that the mayor drinks too much; or when a business journal critiques the performance of a famous CEO; or when an Internet blog asserts that a rock star was lip-synching during a recent concert. It continues to define our rights of public discourse.

31. The Pentagon Papers Case: Balancing National Security against the People's Right to Know

New York Times Co. v. United States (1971)

What happens when a reporter obtains information about an important national issue of great interest to the American people, but the government believes that disclosure of the information would harm national security? Does national security trump a journalist's (or anyone else's) First Amendment right of free speech? If it does, how is it to be determined if the government's national security concerns are genuine, or are really just excuses to avoid political embarrassment?

In 1967, Secretary of Defense Robert S. McNamara commissioned a classified study to disentangle how the United States had become involved in the Vietnam War. The report took more than a year to complete and encompassed forty-seven volumes, with extensive documentary evidence. Later dubbed the "Pentagon Papers," it included evidence that the government had lied to and misled the American people, and that various presidents had overstepped their lawful powers.

Daniel Ellsberg was a Cambridge- and Harvard-educated economist who had served in the military, consulted with the government on key issues such as the Cuban missile crisis, and, having been identified as a rising intellectual resource, was asked to join the Defense Department in 1964 to work for McNamara. In this role, Ellsberg visited Vietnam and observed what he believed were substantial flaws in the development and implementation of United States policy. Ellsberg began to morph from an enthusiastic hawk to a very cynical dove.

From 1967 to 1969, Ellsberg, at McNamara's request, helped to compile the Pentagon Papers, and in the process Ellsberg further confirmed what he saw as rampant governmental deception and misconduct. At the height of his disillusionment, Ellsberg copied substantial portions of the Pentagon Papers and provided them to the press.

The *New York Times* began publishing excerpts from the Pentagon Papers, and the Nixon administration immediately filed a lawsuit, claiming that national security would be compromised if publication continued. Government lawyers successfully obtained an injunction to stop further publication—the first time the government had ever sought an injunction to stop a newspaper from publishing the news. The *New York Times* appealed to the Supreme Court; but in the interim, the *Washington Post* obtained a copy and began publication, resulting in another government lawsuit; the *Boston Globe* then began publication as well. The Supreme Court, recognizing the serious issues involved, expedited the usual procedures, immediately scheduled oral arguments, and just four days later issued its ruling.

Can the President Edit the Evening News?

Decades before, the Supreme Court had ruled that the First Amendment does not permit courts to order a "prior restraint" of free speech, except in the most unusual circumstances. In other words, courts can award damages if what is said or written constitutes libel or slander, and courts can send someone to jail if what is said or written constitutes a crime, but courts cannot, except in the most extraordinary cases, issue orders prohibiting the act of speaking or writing itself.

Owing to the speed with which the case found its way to the Court, the justices issued a joint, very brief opinion reiterating the law regarding prior restraints of speech, stating that the Nixon administration had "a heavy burden of showing justification" for the restraint on the publication of the Pentagon Papers, and concluding that it had not met that burden. The Pentagon Papers were published, and they fueled widespread and accelerating opposition to the Vietnam War, as well as increasing cynicism about government in general.

In addition to this brief statement, several justices of the Court used the case to publish their own lengthy and detailed opinions in which they expressed their views on freedom of the press, and in which they excoriated the government's attempt to stop the publication.

Some justices took the position, consistent with the rulings in some prior cases, that if the publication of certain information would clearly create a direct, immediate, and irreparable injury to the nation, a prior restraint could be issued. Those justices concurred in lifting the injunction against the Pentagon Papers, however, because they felt that the government had not come close to such a showing in the case before the Court.

Other justices, notably Justice Black and Justice Douglas, took the position that the government may never keep information from the public. Justice Black wrote, "In my view, it is unfortunate that some of my Brethren are apparently willing to hold that the publication of news may sometimes be enjoined. Such a holding would make a shambles of the First Amendment." He went on to describe the role the Founding Fathers had envisioned for the press: "The press was to serve the governed, not the governors. The Government's power to censor the press was abolished so that the press would remain forever free to censure the Government. . . . In revealing the workings of government that led to the Vietnam War, the newspapers nobly did precisely that which the Founders hoped and trusted they would do."

Freedom of the Press in a Post–9/11 World

In a post–9/11 world, the conflict between national security and the public's right to know, as exemplified by the Pentagon Papers case, has been heightened. This conflict raises many of the most difficult issues democracies face, and compelling arguments can be made in support of a variety of policy positions. The *New York Times*, for instance, was blessed by some and cursed by others for its exposure in 2005 of the government's previously secret program of domestic electronic eavesdropping, and a multitude of approaches has been suggested by congressmen, senators, and commentators of all parties and political leanings.

However the executive and legislative branches may choose to address these issues in the future, it is unlikely that their decisions will be the last word. The magnificence of a system of government like ours is this: when it works like it's supposed to work, whether the public's right to know has been properly respected by its elected officials is ultimately measured against the requirements of a Constitution that transcends whatever policy preferences may exist at any point in time. And the measuring is to be done by Supreme Court justices with no ax to grind other than the preservation of the core values of the Constitution itself.

CHAPTER 10

OLD LAWS AND NEW TECHNOLOGIES

"Invention is the mother of necessity."

—THORSTEIN VEBLEN, ECONOMIST AND POLITICAL COMMENTATOR

About two hundred years ago, the cotton gin and the steam engine helped change an agricultural society into an industrial society. Mega-factories and a national economy soon followed, and families, workplaces, and governments were forever transformed. In response, a whole new body of laws emerged to address the never-imagined problems new technologies always bring with them. This is how jurisprudence evolves: with each new brainchild, there is always a need for new laws to help resolve new issues.

Yet the Constitution, an eighteenth-century document, remains the fundamental law of our land. How can it apply to twenty-first-century issues? Can an eighteenth-century prohibition against unreasonable searches be sensibly enforced against a twenty-first-century police force? Does the eighteenth-century concept of "free speech" have meaning to the twenty-first-century Internet?

And what happens if the Constitution turns out to be an ancient round peg that simply will not fit within a modern square hole?

A computer board; how will the Constitution adapt to modern technology?

32. Music, Movies, Television, and the Internet

MGM Studios Inc. v. Grokster, Ltd. (2005)
ABC, Inc. v. Aereo, Inc. (2014)

Grokster, and the Advent of "Peer-to-Peer" Technology

Grokster, Ltd. was in the business of distributing free software that allows computer users to share and copy electronic files on a "peer-to-peer" basis—that is, directly from one computer to another computer without having to go through a central server. The Grokster software could be used to share any kind of computer file, but as Grokster well knew, the software was primarily used as a tool to infringe on copyrights—millions of times a month, Grokster users sent copyrighted materials to each other, such as music and video files. The effect was, basically, a high-tech, geometrically multiplied version of what would happen if one person buys a book and then makes thousands of copies and gives them away for free, in violation of the author and publisher's copyright.

To increase its user base, Grokster actively promoted its software as an easy and efficient way to exchange copyrighted music and video files and even offered instructions to users who called the Grokster help line. Grokster was not paid by its users, but as the number of users increased, Grokster generated more advertising revenue.

MGM (along with a group of other copyright holders) sued Grokster for copyright infringement. MGM sought an injunction to stop the use of the Grokster software, and also sought damages from Grokster for the copyright infringements committed by the computer users to whom Grokster distributed its software.

The "Guns Don't Kill People" Defense—Part One

Grokster had some solid defenses—and it won in the lower courts. There was no evidence that Grokster itself ever infringed on a copyright, and it was not contested that, for instance, students and business executives who wanted an efficient way to exchange word processing files or spreadsheets could and did use Grokster for completely legal purposes. Grokster contended that it could not be held responsible if users chose to employ its software for illegal purposes—the technological equivalent of the "guns don't kill people, people kill people" defense.

In fact, there was solid legal precedent for Grokster's position. In 1975, Sony introduced the first widely available VCR, known as the Betamax, and in 1976, Universal Studios and the Walt Disney Company sued Sony for "contributory infringement." Sony, they contended, was selling a device that its customers could use to copy copyrighted television shows, which they could charge others to view, or which they could recopy and sell.

The case made a tortured journey through the courts, ultimately resulting in the Supreme Court's 1984 landmark decision. The Supreme Court likened the Betamax to a copy machine—selling a copy machine does not constitute contributory infringement just because the copy machine *could* be used for unlawful purposes; the test is whether "the product is widely used for legitimate, unobjectionable purposes." The Court found that at least "one potential use of the Betamax plainly satisfies this standard, however it is understood: private, noncommercial time-shifting in the home," which enables a viewer to see at a later time a copyrighted television show the viewer has the absolute right to see. That sort of wholly lawful use of the Betamax "should not be stifled simply because the equipment is used by some individuals to make unauthorized reproductions" of the show. When *MGM Studios Inc. v. Grokster, Ltd.* got to the Supreme Court, Grokster made the same argument about its software that Sony had made about the Betamax—but unlike Sony, Grokster lost. What was the difference?

The Supreme Court decided that even though Grokster made a product that, like the VCR, could be used for lawful purposes, Grokster had "induced" its customers to use its product for unlawful purposes, and Grokster should be held liable for that unlawful inducement. It was as if Grokster sold an electric screwdriver, but advertised and supported it as a means to pick locks and commit burglaries. The Supreme Court made it clear that "mere knowledge" of the fact that a product was being used unlawfully would not be enough to create liability. Sony, for instance, knew that some customers used VCRs unlawfully. But Sony marketed VCRs as a device to be used for lawful purposes, such as time shifting. Grokster, on the other hand, energetically encouraged its users to take a product that could be used lawfully and use it unlawfully; that was the difference between being liable and not being liable.

Grokster was out of business.

Aereo, and the Changes in Broadcast Technology

In the late 1940s and early 1950s, the Community Antenna Television industry—known as CATV—was born. The idea was to better serve communities situated in hilly areas, where receipt of broadcast signals was difficult. Enterprising companies placed an antenna on a hill above these communities and, for a fee, transmitted television signals to homes in the area through coaxial cables. As might be imagined, the networks were not happy and wanted a piece of that action.

The networks got the better of the lobbying efforts that followed. In 1976, Congress overhauled copyright law and included a provision in the new law known as the "Transmit Clause." The law made it unlawful to "publicly perform" a copyrighted work, and the Transmit

Clause defined "publicly perform" to include transmissions of a copyrighted work "by means of any device or process, whether the members of the public capable of receiving the performance or display receive it in the same place or in separate places and at the same time or at different times." Simultaneous translation: if you obtain a copyrighted television show and then, through whatever means, transmit it to members of the public, you have violated the copyright law and will be liable for substantial damages. Congress nailed down that requirement even further in subsequent legislation that regulated the activities of cable companies.

This gave birth to the cable television industry as we know it today. The cable companies can obtain all manner of copyrighted broadcast television content and sell it to cable subscribers, but in order to do so, the cable companies have to pay a hefty fee to the broadcasters, which the cable companies pass on to their subscribers. The point is that the companies that own the copyrights on the shows have the right to get paid by anyone who broadcasts the shows.

Enter a new company with an innovative new technology, Aereo, Inc. Founded in 2012, Aereo produced extremely small—the size of a coin—antennae which could capture and digitize over-the-air broadcasts. Each Aereo subscriber was individually assigned its own antenna and disk space, which were maintained by Aereo in its facilities. The subscriber could use the antenna and disk space to access and record over-the-air broadcasts, and the subscriber could then watch these recorded television programs over the Internet, using a computer, smart phone, tablet, or any other Internet-connected device, whenever and wherever the subscriber preferred.

Several networks sued Aereo, claiming copyright infringement—Aereo, they claimed, was the modern, high-tech equivalent of the cable television companies. Cable companies are required to pay monumental licensing fees to the networks for their transmission of the networks' over-the-air broadcast to their customers, and Aereo was no different.

The "Guns Don't Kill People" Defense—Part Two

Not so, said Aereo. Aereo pointed out that the Transmit Clause only applies to companies that rebroadcast over-the-air shows to *members of the public*, and that is *not* what Aereo did. Rather than being a broadcaster, Aereo acts just like a VCR—it provides a technology that allows a subscriber to select and record for later viewing an over-the-air television show that the subscriber had the absolute right to view for free— the subscriber could have erected an antenna, watched the show, or recorded it on a VCR and watched it later. What's the meaningful difference between that and the technology Aereo provides?

By the letter of the law, Aereo was right, but by a 6–3 majority, the Supreme Court was not willing to rule based on words written by Congress in 1976; recognizing that Congress could not have foreseen the technologies that would surface almost forty years later, the Court attempted to apply Congress's logic and intent, if not its specific phraseology. "Aereo's activities are substantially similar to those of the CATV companies" that Congress had in mind, and Aereo's "behind-the-scenes" technological differences did not change the fact that Aereo's "commercial objective" is the same as that of a cable company, and the Aereo customers' "viewing experience" is largely the same as if Aereo were a cable company. The conclusion: "Congress would as much have intended to protect a copyright holder from the unlicensed activities of Aereo as from those of cable companies."

Aereo, like Grokster, folded shortly thereafter.

Protecting Rights Versus Encouraging Innovation

Grokster and *Aereo* are excellent examples of what happens when the Supreme Court confronts twenty-first-century technologies that prior lawmakers could not have foreseen. Ultimately, the law's job is to reflect society's views on what is fair and just. When faced with conduct that may conform with the letter but not the spirit of prior laws, as when new technologies circumvent the rights of patent and copyright holders to the fruits of their labor, capital, and creativity, the Supreme Court must make the difficult choice of either mechanically applying the law as it exists while waiting for the legislature to enact new laws, or tweaking the law so that the results comport with established notions of justice.

But there is another side to that coin. Many high-tech companies require hundreds of thousands, if not millions, of dollars, to get a new product or service off the ground. Before risking their money, investors will carefully research the prospects for success, and as part of that process, they will engage lawyers to determine if the proposed product or service will violate the law. The lawyers will look at the law and provide an opinion, as they no doubt did in respect to the Grokster and Aereo projects. The *Grokster* and *Aereo* decisions send the message that many risks worth taking in the past may not be worth taking in the future—who knows the extent to which the courts may stretch old laws to cover new technologies? And that message may stem the tide of the innovation that drives economic and social advances.

The *Aereo* Court realized that and sent a lukewarm assurance that the *Aereo* decision might not apply to other situations. "We cannot now answer more precisely how the Transmit Clause or other provisions of the Copyright Act will apply to technologies not before us." That is not so much a message to future innovators as it is a message to Congress to clarify or rewrite existing laws so that those who wish to pursue new technologies can determine before, and not just after, whether their efforts are legal or illegal.

33. How Much Privacy Are You Entitled to in a High-Tech World?

Kyllo v. United States (2001)

Unlike the implied right of privacy on which the *Griswold* and *Roe* cases discussed previously were based, there is an explicit right of privacy plainly expressed in the Fourth Amendment to the Constitution. That provision restricts the right of the government to snoop into the personal affairs of Americans through the admonition that the "right of the people to be secure in their persons, houses, papers, and effects, against unreasonable searches and seizures, shall not be violated." If the government wants to conduct a search, the Fourth Amendment mandates that it must go to a judge and obtain a warrant "upon probable cause, supported by Oath or affirmation, and particularly describing the place to be searched and the persons or things to be seized."

But how much privacy does the Fourth Amendment actually provide in a high-tech world, where the FBI and even the local police have electronic devices and computer capabilities that can do what the framers of the Constitution could not possibly have imagined?

Federal agents were suspicious that Danny Lee Kyllo was growing marijuana in his home. The agents secretly set up a thermal-imaging device outside the Kyllo home in order to determine if the heat emanating from the home was consistent with the high-intensity lamps typically used to nurture indoor marijuana plants. The scan showed that Kyllo's garage roof and a side wall were relatively hot compared to the rest of his home and were substantially warmer than neighboring homes. On the basis of that information, the agents obtained a warrant, searched Kyllo's home, found growing marijuana plants, and convicted Kyllo on a federal drug charge.

Kyllo argued that his conviction should be overturned because the government's use of the thermal-imaging device to detect what was going on inside his house was "an unreasonable search and seizure" that violated his rights under the Fourth Amendment. Still, how could that be? All the government did was monitor what was going on outside Kyllo's house.

Can You "Search" a House Without Ever Going Inside?

Over many years, the Supreme Court has developed a body of rules that flesh out the meaning of the Fourth Amendment. At their core, these rules mandate that citizens are entitled to privacy within their homes, and that the only way the police can invade that privacy is by going to a judge, demonstrating the need to invade that privacy, and obtaining a warrant. There are some limited exceptions, such as true emergencies. But other than that, our homes are our castles, and the government's right to intrude into our homes requires a warrant.

Kyllo's situation presented another example of what happens when eighteenth-century laws meet twenty-first-century technology. What happens if, using the latest electronic and computer capabilities, the authorities can look inside your home without ever getting close to your front door, and without your even knowing they are in the neighborhood? Does the Fourth Amendment prohibit the government from analyzing what is happening outside a house in order to determine what is going on inside the house?

Kyllo lost his case in the lower courts, and the Supreme Court agreed to hear his appeal. Most commentators believe that since at least the 1990s, the Supreme Court has favored law enforcement authorities, and in the process has relaxed many of the rights afforded to those who commit or are accused of committing crimes. Therefore, the presumption was that Kyllo's argument would be viewed with disdain and that the Supreme Court would use the case as a means to put another arrow in law enforcement's quiver.

Privacy Trumps Technology

It did not turn out that way. Kyllo won. In the process, the Supreme Court began the effort to set limits on "Big Brother" that will help to further define twenty-first-century privacy rights.

The Supreme Court ruled that unless the government gets a warrant, it cannot use a device that is not in general public use to effectively look inside a private home from the outside: if the police would need a warrant to go into the house to find out what was going on inside, they must get a warrant to accomplish the same result using high-tech devices from outside the house. In years past, the Supreme Court had ruled that the government can, without a warrant, use binoculars to look through the windows of a house (or even fly overhead) to see what is in plain view. But the *Kyllo* Court ruled that other than that, citizens have the right to expect what's inside their homes to remain private, and that right of privacy is violated just as much by a police officer crawling through a window as it is by the use of technology to accomplish the same result. The message was clear: If the police want to see what's not in plain view inside a private home, they need a warrant.

There are a myriad of technology-versus-privacy issues that the Supreme Court has not yet had the opportunity to address, and *Kyllo* may be a key indicator of the direction in which the Supreme Court will head. For instance, the government has reportedly developed a technology through which it can e-mail a program to a suspect's computer and then monitor the suspect's computer keystrokes. Isn't this a way to peer inside a home from outside the home, and wouldn't the logic of *Kyllo* require overenthusiastic government agents to first obtain a warrant?

What about homeowners who use wireless computer networks? Wireless network signals can be picked up from outside a home. Could local police who think you may be conducting illegal activities in your house set up on the public street outside your home, tap into your wireless network, monitor your e-mails, and search your hard drive?

In 2012, the Court decided *United States v. Jones*, a case in which police, acting without a warrant, installed a GPS tracking device on a suspected drug dealer's car, secretly tracked the suspect's whereabouts for twenty-eight days, and used that evidence to convict him. A unanimous Court ruled that this constituted an unlawful search and reversed the conviction. But while they all aligned on the ultimate result, the justices wrote an array of individual opinions and strongly disagreed on *why* the police conduct was unlawful—they struggled to fit the concept of GPS technology into Fourth Amendment precedents that were centuries old. Was it that the police physically attached the device to Jones's car, and there would have been no issue if they had used some other type of remote monitoring? Was it that they tracked Jones for an extended time, as opposed to just a day or two?

In *Kyllo*, the Court stated its intent to protect fundamental rights against the end runs that new technologies can provide to government authorities. For citizens concerned about their rights of privacy, *Kyllo* is a first step in an important direction. But just how far the Court will go, and whether it will be able to formulate a consistent approach to new technologies, is far from clear.

For example, in *Jones*, Justice Alito highlighted some of the difficult issues that were not yet decided. "In some locales," Justice Alito wrote, "closed-circuit television video monitoring is becoming ubiquitous. On toll roads, automatic toll collection systems create a precise record of the movements of motorists who choose to make use of that convenience. Many motorists purchase cars that are equipped with devices that permit a central station to ascertain the car's location at any time so that roadside assistance may be provided if needed and the car may be found if it is stolen." There is no consensus on when, or whether, the police may obtain and use this information without obtaining a warrant. And the issues will become even more difficult when layered over emerging law-enforcement challenges, such as stopping the spate of mass shooting incidents the nation has endured and the national security issues inherent in the war against global terrorism.

34. Do the Police Have the Right to Search Your Cell Phone?

Riley v. California (2014)

Since the Bill of Rights was adopted in 1791, the Fourth Amendment has mandated that, absent a true emergency situation, the police have to get a warrant before they can search you, your possessions, your desk, your house, or anything else that belongs to you—that is, they have to prove to a judge that there is a good reason why they ought to be permitted to conduct the search.

However, approximately a century ago, an exception began to take shape, and in many respects that exception came to dominate the rule: if the police are in the midst of making an arrest, they are permitted to make a "search incident to arrest" on the spot, without a warrant. Basically (there are some twists and turns), the "search incident to arrest" rule means that the police can search anything in your pockets, on your person, or within your reach. The logic of the rule is twofold: first, the police have the right to protect themselves, and can search for weapons; second, the police have the right to prevent the person they are arresting from destroying evidence that might be within grabbing distance.

So, let's suppose you are stopped for a traffic violation. The police officer notices a purse on the seat next to you, and he demands that you turn it over to him. He opens your purse and sees a cell phone. He scrolls through the e-mails and photos on your cell phone—where he finds an e-mail between you and a friend confirming an illegal marijuana purchase, and some selfies of you and your underage brother smoking an unknown substance. You are handcuffed, put in the police car, and transported to the police station.

That is the way the "search incident to arrest" rule worked—until June 25, 2014, when the Supreme Court decided *Riley v. California*.

There was just one issue the *Riley* Court had to rule on. As stated by Chief Justice Roberts, who wrote on behalf of a unanimous Court, the case required the justices "to decide how the search incident to arrest doctrine applies to modern cell phones, which are now such a pervasive and insistent part of daily life that the proverbial visitor from Mars might conclude they were an important feature of human anatomy."

The Chief Justice then answered the question as directly as it could be answered: "Our answer to the question of what police must do before searching a cell phone seized incident to an arrest is accordingly simple—get a warrant." In other words, the "search incident to arrest" rule will no longer apply to cell phones.

A Break with the Past:
More New Rules for More New Technologies

In reaching this decision, the Court emphatically stressed that the search of a cell phone is vastly different than a search of a wallet, a purse, a notebook, an envelope, or whatever else might be in reach. Here is how Chief Justice Roberts put it: First, a cell phone collects in one place many distinct types of information—an address, a note, a prescription, a bank statement, a video—that reveal much more in combination than any isolated record. Second, a cell phone's capacity allows even just one type of information to convey far more than previously possible. The sum of an individual's private life can be reconstructed through a thousand photographs labeled with dates, locations, and descriptions; the same cannot be said of a photograph or two of loved ones tucked into a wallet. Third, the data on a phone can date back to the purchase of the phone, or even earlier. A person might carry in his pocket a slip of paper reminding him to call Mr. Jones; he would not carry a record of all his communications with Mr. Jones for the past several months, as would routinely be kept on a phone.

The Justice Department had argued that cell phones were not materially different from wallets, purses, and address books. Chief Justice Roberts replied, "That is like saying a ride on horseback is materially indistinguishable from a flight to the moon."

Chief Justice Roberts then explained why the usual rationales for the "search incident to an arrest" rule did not apply to cell phones. In addition to the obvious fact that a police officer need not search a cell phone for self-protective purposes, he explained that an immediate search of cell phone data would not prevent the destruction of evidence—for example, a message from another electronic device could "wipe" cell phone data at any time, and rather than conducting a search of the cell phone data, the better solution would be to remove the cell phone battery or place the cell phone in an environment where it could not receive remote signals.

The *Riley* decision does not mean that a police officer cannot seize a cell phone during the course of a lawful arrest. It only means that (except in emergencies and assuming the owner of the cell phone does not give consent) the police officer cannot search it at that time—and, more significantly, it means that the police can never search it unless they could first convince a judge that there was a reason to do so and that a warrant should be issued. Mere curiosity or speculation will not do.

After *Riley*, the police could no more break into your cell phone without a warrant than they could break into your home without a warrant.

It's Not Just About Cell Phones . . .

For the 12 million people arrested every year—many for traffic stops or minor offenses—*Riley* is very big news. But *Riley*'s significance will extend much further than cell phones seized in the course of an arrest.

Riley is the first Supreme Court case specifically dealing with the application of the Fourth Amendment to digital data—and the Court could not have been more emphatic in concluding that modern cell phones, which are nothing but minicomputers, are a completely different storage medium to which the old rules cannot be applied. There is every reason to believe that the *Riley* ruling will be applied to government searches of tablets, laptops, hard drives, remote servers, and other data storage devices—and, before too long, the refrain "Hey, you, get off of my cloud" will likely have new meaning.

Time will tell if the *Riley* rationale will be applied in other contexts, outside of the criminal law, where privacy is at issue. Privacy advocates will doubtlessly argue that, for example, the *Riley* logic should limit the rights of employers to access employee e-mails and other data. The fact that all nine of the Supreme Court justices voted in favor of *Riley* evidences the Court's appreciation of the privacy issues inherent in digital media, and it is fair to assume that *Riley*'s break with the past will lead to a significant, if unpredictable, future.

AFTERWORD

Our goal must be to remain the "government of laws, not men" that our Founding Fathers envisioned. But for so long as men have the power to change the laws, achieving that goal will require persistent vigilance.

Democracy American-Style

Here's the way it's supposed to work. Democracy American-style means that government—Congress, the president, or the local town council— can do what they think best concerning the laws they enact and the actions they take. But, all the while, they know that the Supreme Court lurks in the background, reserving the right to sound the alarm if constitutional boundaries are violated. In this way, our system deters and defeats those who would seek to convert our government of laws into a government of men who substitute their own judgments and interests for our fundamental constitutional freedoms and guaranties. The Supreme Court serves as the Constitution's whistleblower.

Great theory . . . except, as the foregoing chapters have hopefully made plain, the Supreme Court is itself made up of men and women who may seek to substitute their own views or political preferences for the Constitution's mandates; and, even when acting in the utmost good faith, their actions are colored by their own foibles, backgrounds, and opinions. The Supreme Court has the power to police the constitutional compliance of the executive and the legislature, but who polices the Supreme Court?

Given the Supreme Court's power, it can be disconcerting to admit, as we must, that Supreme Court justices, like all humans, are fallible, they have ingrained philosophical biases, and they are subject to political pressures. Moreover, even the most supreme of justices, like all humans, see the world through the lens of the events and norms of their times. Many of the Supreme Court cases discussed previously make this all too plain. The Fourteenth Amendment, for instance, assures "equal protection" and, indeed, "Equal Justice Under Law" is literally carved in stone over the entrance to the Supreme Court itself. Yet for decades, highly respected Supreme Court justices consistently deemed "separate but equal" racial segregation constitutionally acceptable. That precept was ultimately reversed, but it was not reversed because the words in the Constitution changed. It was reversed because different justices raised in a different era and informed by different social values knew it to be wrong—but it took fifty years to happen.

How can a country, let alone a judicial system, function when that which the highest court in the land finds to be a constitutional certainty on one day becomes a constitutional anachronism on the next?

"The Worst Form of Government . . ."

Yet when the array of checks, balances, and interrelationships is dispassionately analyzed, the most remarkable part is this: despite its undeniable failures and foibles, our system works better than the Constitution's framers could have hoped.

The reason for this success lies not just in the design of the system; it also lies in the qualifications and integrity of the people who have served within the system. The axiomatic lesson to be drawn from that reality must never be ignored or forgotten.

The vast majority of those selected to serve on the Supreme Court have been men and women of utmost good faith and open mind who, despite their differences in judicial and political philosophies and life views, treated the Constitution with awestruck reverence. In addition, the Court has produced a pantheon of social and judicial thinkers of extraordinary wisdom—Holmes, Cardozo, Brandeis, Frankfurter, and many more—who perceived the system's weaknesses and pitfalls, and skillfully navigated the country around and through them. The inherent fluidity of the law has only rarely been used to promote personal agendas, and has instead served as a self-correcting mechanism that allows the law to adjust over time to emerging realities.

The result has been the creation of an astounding body of law that has both reflected, and directed, the changing social and cultural landscape of our country. Justice Oliver Wendell Holmes Jr. put it best. "The life of the law," he said, "has not been logic; it has been experience." The way in which the Supreme Court has utilized the experiences of the country, and itself, to channel the law and, in turn, the way we live and function is astonishing.

Clearly, there is room for substantial disagreement over the wisdom of many Supreme Court decisions. It has often taken much too long for injustices to be remedied. In hindsight it is plain that serious, sometimes damaging, errors have been made. But when the whole of the Supreme Court's two centuries of work is reviewed and assessed, it is difficult not to be enthralled. It has become a cliché to remark, as did Winston Churchill, that "democracy is the worst form of government except for all those others that have been tried." In this country, the Supreme Court can take much pride in the cliché's continuing life as a demonstrable truth.

Inventing the Future

In the coming years, the Supreme Court will face daunting issues that have as much to do with philosophy, ethics, politics, and economics as with legal interpretations. Depending on how activist an approach the Supreme Court chooses to undertake, it can literally redefine the workings of government, the electoral process, the war on terrorism, the responsibilities of business, the place of religion, the nature of the family, the approach to climate change, and a host of other issues that will determine how Americans live and work.

The Supreme Court has defined much of our past. We now live in an era in which the Supreme Court is, in fundamental ways, inventing our future.

It has its flaws. It has made mistakes. But, still, no governmental institution is better suited to the task. Should there come a time when that is no longer the case—a time when the Supreme Court is influenced more by politics than foundational principles, a time when we fail to function as a government of laws, and not men—we will no longer be the nation we are supposed to be, the nation that others strive to become.

INDEX

Note: Page numbers in *italics* include illustrations and photographs.

PHOTO CREDITS